Gift of Life

Gift of Life

A
Spiritual Companion
for the Mother-to-Be

by Joan Swirsky

Daybreak™ Books
A Division of Rodale Press, Inc.
Emmaus, Pennsylvania

Copyright © 1997 by Joan Swirsky
Daybreak is a trademark of Rodale Press, Inc.

Printed in the United States of America on acid-free ∞, recycled paper ♲

Cover and Book Designer: Kristen Morgan Downey

Cover Photograph: Allison Mitsch

Library of Congress Cataloging-in-Publication Data
Swirsky, Joan.
    Gift of Life: a spiritual companion for the mother-to-be / by Joan Swirsky.
    p.   cm.
    ISBN 0-87596-427-3   hardcover
    1. Pregnant women—Religious life. 2. Pregnancy—Religious apects. 3. Mothers—Religious life. 4. Motherhood—Religious aspects. I. Title.
    BL625. 7. S85 1997
    291.4'41—DC21   96-46658

Distributed in the book trade by St. Martin's Press

2   4   6   8   10   9   7   5   3   1   hardcover

—— OUR PURPOSE ——

*"We publish books that empower
people's minds and spirits."*

This book is dedicated

to my husband, Steve,
who taught me everything about love;

to my three children—Seth, David, and Karen—
who taught me the great lessons of life;

and to my grandson Julian,
who embodies the miracle of life itself.

Contents

Contents

Contents

Acknowledgments

Eternal praise and appreciation to my mother, Gertrude Krevit Finkle, who taught me to love the spoken and written word and who, by bringing me into the world, gave me the greatest of God's gifts—life.

To my agent, Denise Stinson, my deep thanks for introducing me to Karen Kelly and helping both of us to launch this special project.

To Karen Kelly, my inspired editor, who guided this volume with love and wisdom, my deep appreciation.

To Carol Weiss, my always encouraging friend and astute adviser, deepest thanks.

To Elana Hayden, great love and heartfelt gratitude for her valued friendship and always-wise advice.

To Reine Stempa, my gratitude for sharing her historical erudition and evolved spirituality.

To Florence Rapoport, my literate and generous friend, thank you.

And to Joseph Attie, M.D., artist of camera and scalpel, my eternal thanks.

Introduction

At 18, I gave birth to my first child. During my ninth month, I remember looking down at my huge girth and thinking, "I'm going to die." Even though I knew how babies were born, I simply couldn't imagine how this big baby was going to find his way out of me.

After ingesting a distinctly unappetizing concoction of orange juice and castor oil—the way babies were induced in the early 1960s—I entered the hospital, taking special notice of everyone and everything that met my gaze. I was really quite sure that I would be seeing all of them for the last time.

As the labor progressed and I heard the wails of other women in labor, I felt isolated and scared. When a resident came to check me, I asked him only to hold my hand. Twelve hours later, my son came into the world.

Although exhausted from the labor, I remember hearing his cries and feeling a great surge of personal power. At that moment I knew that the awesome act of childbirth was life's most important event. It changed my life forever.

At the time, I was living on a college campus where my husband was a student. When I watched him and his classmates rushing off to school, I wondered what they would possibly do with their lives that could equal the importance of bringing a life into the world and then nurturing it. I still can't think of anything that compares to this ultimate creative act.

I gave birth again at 20 and 23, both thrilling experiences that equaled the first (but with less fear). In all three childbirth experiences the greatest help I received was not from the books I read nor the doctors I saw but from my trust that Mother Nature had perfectly designed my body for this magnificent task and from my belief in an all-knowing God. These beliefs continued to guide me through my life.

As time went on, I became an obstetrical nurse, childbirth instructor, and psychotherapist. I met and spoke with hundreds of women who had faithfully attended their doctors' appointments, diligently taken their childbirth classes, heroically juggled domestic responsibilities with demanding careers, and studiously learned everything possible about their pregnancies. But one thing always seemed to be absent: the spiritual aspect of this life-affirming experience, the recognition of God's presence in the miracle of life.

Instead of speaking only of the clinical aspects of pregnancy and childbirth—the first missed period, the transforming body (and body image), the ruptured membranes, the bloody show, the dilating cervix, the list goes on—*Gift of Life* discusses the profound collaboration of mother and father in translating the twinkle in their eyes to the conception of their baby and the overwhelmingly mysterious processes that guide pregnancy and childbirth.

Here, you will also read of the deep and irrevocable spiritual bond that is shared by mother and baby and the mutual voyage they embark on as both of them struggle to actualize the birth and meet each other for the very first time.

It is my hope that this book will accompany women (and their partners) in their daily lives and help them to locate the spiritual center within themselves—to their own, their family's, and their child's immense and long-lasting benefit.

Spiritual—What Does That Mean?

God, the Universe, and You

On a sultry summer day you decide to escape to the beach. As you stand at the water's edge, while barefoot as a carefree child, you feel a rolling carpet of grainy, sun-kissed sand beneath your toes. All around you soar snowy white seagulls, swooping and cawing, dancing on the water with ballerina grace. You inhale the salty air and are filled with a feeling of cleanness, of purity.

Your eyes search the horizon. There, for as far as you can see, is the never-ending ocean, still and calm or roaring with white-capped waves. Your eyes wander upward, and you behold the sky's immense expanse—clear, blue, without end. Almost unconsciously, you begin to contemplate the vastness of the universe.

"The ocean has been here forever," you think, "and the

sky." You marvel when you imagine the vibrant life of plants and fish that exists in the dark, mysterious depths of the ocean, at the survival skills of the seemingly fragile birds that glide above. You gaze at clouds of filmy organza wafting elegantly overhead, and you smile secretly to yourself as you interpret their cryptic patterns. You close your eyes and feel your face caressed by a sweet, gentle breeze.

All at once, you feel swept away with awe and emotion and appreciation. Away from your hectic everyday life, you can view your own place in the measureless universe with perspective. You can even laugh at many of the things that you thought had momentous importance just a few hours before. As your cares and anxieties melt away, you can value the moment, knowing that you are in the presence of something greater than yourself, something ancient and enduring, something wise and loving.

For many, this "something" is God. For others, it is nature. For most, it is both. In any case you have just had a spiritual experience. You have recognized a dimension of the cosmos that we all inhabit as being majestic—larger and more mysterious than can be comprehended by man or woman, poet or sage, scientist or philosopher. It is a wonderful experience. Freeing, comforting, deep, insightful.

Yet, the spiritual forces that you have just experienced—the spirit of the world and of yourself—cannot easily be defined. They cannot be seen or touched. They do not have a distinctive scent or a recognizable sound. Deriving from the biblical concept of "the breath of wind," the spirit is not material nor tangible, but rather ageless and eternal.

"Let There Be Light"

The poet Virgil said that "the spirit within nourishes." Paul the Apostle said that it was ". . .of power, and of love. . ." In Galatians: "The fruit of the Spirit is love, joy, peace. . .gentleness, goodness, faith." And the first page of the Old Testament pronounces that "the spirit of God moved upon the face of the waters. And God said, Let there be light, and there was light." Yes, the spirit is the light within each of us, a luminous presence that serves as a beacon of wisdom and as a benevolent guide.

Spirituality is that part of the human experience that is pure and sacred, that cannot be touched by the profane influences of everyday life. Once acknowledged and embraced, the spirit of life nourishes by permeating every cell of the body, the mind, and the heart. From within, it warms the chill in our bones. It sweetens bitter tears. It soothes the empty spaces of isolation like quiet velvet. It places the million jigsaw pieces of life in perfect order. And it does all these things, and more, with wisdom and with love.

Certainly, having a wonderful day at the beach is an uplifting—and spiritual—experience. You may have expressed your feelings about it in words, telling a friend or loved one of this "perfect" interlude, but the deep, knowing, transcendent part of your experience—the part in which you felt the immensity of God's presence—may have left you speechless.

No doubt you resolved to carry these magical moments with you into your busy, demanding life. But, alas, the glow of such moments usually doesn't last. Real life intrudes upon your resolve, and you find yourself dreaming about the beach, fantasizing about the sanctuary that you found among the sand and the surf and the seagulls, longing to recapture the peace and joy that you felt during those enchanted moments.

Am I a Spiritual Person?

Of course, spiritual experiences don't have to start and end at the beach, or in any other away-from-it-all spot. The wonders of the universe are everywhere, waiting to be noticed, challenging us to partake of their riches.

Our spiritual selves are an intrinsic part of us, although it is also true that we spend less time focusing on this part of our lives than we do on just about anything else. For the most part, we go through our lives believing that if we learn as much as we can about the material world—our bodies, our education, our jobs, ad infinitum—we will be in control and able to contend with life's challenges.

But is that true? After all, we are just beginning to learn of the potential that our genes play in determining who we are, what talents or strengths we may inherit, and to which diseases we are vulnerable. From which ancestor did those deep-set dimples come? Our hair color, our aptitude for mathematics, our temperament, our musical ability? While we may be able to trace this or that characteristic to an uncle or sister or parent or grandparent, we still don't understand the mysterious mechanisms that account for it all.

Our minds present an even greater enigma. Who can say exactly what the ingredients are of the still-uncharted territories that Freud so painstakingly began to map more than a century ago? Does the unconscious appear on diagnostic tests? No. Can the ego, the id, and the superego be visualized? No. Can the brains and minds of geniuses or criminals be differentiated in any significant ways? Not at all. Actually, we are far from understanding the complex workings of the mind in any deep, comprehensive, meaningful, and relevant manner.

The same may be true of spirituality, but this facet of human existence has been with us for a much longer time. Long before sonograms and amniocentesis, and long before the study of psychology, people had babies, trusting that the all-knowing help of God and nature, along with their caretakers, would protect them, lead them in the right direction, and instruct them on how to proceed. The survival of our species over these many millennia is testimony to that faith.

You may be a person who is religious in an orthodox,

ritualistic sense, attending the services of your religion, celebrating its holidays, and holding within you a clear picture of God. Or you may believe in God but have no attraction for the rituals of your faith.

But, whatever relationship you have to God and religion, you still have a spiritual center, a place where the material world cannot intrude, a core that places you in the context of the vast universe, with all of its history, triumphs, tragedies, and mysteries. That core is a place of wisdom, one that sets all of life's vicissitudes in proper perspective and, by doing so, elevates the everyday business of living to a higher, more meaningful plane.

All people, religious or not, yearn deeply to know peace, to understand the great forces of nature, to experience what the ancient sages described as the power of the spirit to endow us with love, goodness, and faith. It is significant that God's first words were "Let there be light." This, above all, is what all people long for, a way to come out of the darkness of ignorance and into the shining light of wisdom. When you tap into your spiritual nature, this brilliant light will illuminate your own life.

Spirituality and the Modern Woman

But how is spirituality relevant to having a baby? After all, childbirth and the conception and pregnancy that precede it are all quintessentially physical acts. Of course, there is also a large emotional component to these significant and highly charged events—but spiritual?

Is conceiving a child uplifting? Does pregnancy lead to insight? Does the arduousness of hard labor fill one with thoughts of a higher power? And does pushing a baby through a birth canal result in a transforming experience?

Actually, many, if not most, women consider childbirth an event that lies in the realm of the miraculous. But for most, the experience is so fraught with physical and emotional ups and downs that the spiritual aspect gets lost in the shuffle, with prayer and meditation called upon only when emergencies arise.

That is not surprising, given the nature of modern life. While plenty of women still have babies in their teens and twenties, with many living "traditional" lives in which mommies stay home and daddies go to work, today more women have their first babies in their thirties, and many even in their early forties.

A great number of these women delay marriage and motherhood in order to finish college, often to earn higher degrees, and to establish themselves in careers. They lead lives very unlike those that their mothers led. Rather than marrying early and making home and motherhood their main pursuits, many modern women spend years living in their own homes or apartments and supporting themselves while they scale the competitive ladder of success.

When they do marry, it is with the understanding that they and their partners will be a two-career family. While this brave new world has many advantages, it also requires adjustments that couples of yesteryear were not called upon to make. The sheer busyness of their separate time schedules and the juggling of domestic responsibilities make the time that they spend with each other a top priority, but one not always easy to manage. Sometimes, everything feels rushed, including lovemaking.

Pregnancy itself has changed. In the past, having children guaranteed that ignorance about pregnancy and childbirth was indeed bliss. Today, women are so saturated with information, so assailed by predelivery sonograms, challenge tests, and amniocenteses, that "knowing" becomes overwhelming. Between agonizing over test results and managing the demands of careers and marriages, they are often too busy to pay attention to much else. Certainly, spirituality lies in this neglected realm.

In addition, modern women rarely fit the stereotype of "mother" that prevailed in the past. Today, increasing numbers of women are single mothers, either by choice or through divorce or widowhood. With few exceptions, their lives are complicated by finding suitable caretakers for their children, by financial concerns, and by plain old fatigue.

Even though most modern women find the time to read numerous books and how-to guides about pregnancy and childbirth, to attend their childbirth-preparation classes, and even to decorate their child-to-be's nursery, many miss the truly exhilarating rewards that spirituality offers. But it doesn't have to be that way. The spiritual aspect of pregnancy (from lovemaking to conception to birth), the aspect that places this most awesome of acts in its proper context—the rightness of and the oneness with nature and God—is available to every mother-to-be and her partner.

This is not to recommend that women abandon their schedules to meditate on a mountaintop. Nor does it suggest that women get any more or less religious than they already are. The wonderful thing about spirituality is that it requires nothing more than a willingness to look at the events of your life in a new way, to tap into your intrinsic wellspring of wisdom, and to use your new vision to embrace all the facets of your life with renewed appreciation.

"It's a Miracle!"

Just think about the people you know who have had a baby. Or yourself, if you have had a baby. After conceiving the child, carrying it through a pregnancy, negotiating labor, and delivering that child, what does every parent say? "It's a miracle!" New mothers forget about the nausea, labor, and pain once their babies are placed in their arms.

Instinctively, they know that something greater than any physical or even emotional process was involved. That "something" is what spirituality is all about: the acknowledgment that all of us are influenced by a presence that we don't really understand, but before which we stand in awe.

Throughout recorded history, it has always been this way. Early cave drawings depict the revered place in which pregnant women and birth were held. The Old Testament celebrates Eve, Sarah, Rachel, Leah, Rebekah, and Hannah. The New Testament exalts Mary and the miracle of her virgin birth. Greek myths speak of the power and wondrousness of Demeter, the maternal goddess.

Through the ages poets and musicians have waxed poetic and melodious about motherhood. Samuel Taylor Coleridge said that a mother was "the holiest thing alive." And Sigmund Freud, albeit controversially, placed mothers at the very center of human experience. Yes, the act of giving birth inspires wonder and amazement and, by its sheer incomprehensible nature, honors the unfathomable powers of God and of nature.

Certainly, then, the wondrous act of conceiving a baby is also worthy of a spiritual response. How inspiring and at the same time humbling it is to contemplate the ability of a solitary egg to unite with an equally solitary sperm to form the beginning of a human life.

How mind-boggling it is that these two infinitesimal cells divide and multiply with such precision that they ultimately develop into perfectly formed blood vessels, ears, knees, a heart, a brain, a mind, a mop of curly hair, one-of-a-kind fingerprints, distinctive features, and the potential to become a perfect human being—perhaps the next Einstein or Mozart or, more commonly, variations of our own quite extraordinary selves. And how important it is to praise God and nature for these marvels.

Why Wait?

But why wait until conception has taken place to embark on your spiritual journey? Unlike the transitory changes that pregnancy will require—the consumption of prenatal vitamins or the juggling of appointments—spirituality will enrich your life every day and last forever.

So even before you conceive, when you are just considering becoming a parent, is the time to embrace spirituality. When conception takes place and pregnancy follows, spirituality will enhance these life-affirming events and add a dimension to your life that will bode well for a positive and harmonious experience.

"But I'm already pregnant," you may say, or "I'm practically ready to give birth." It's never too late to start your spiritual venture. One of the wonderful things about spirituality is that its welcoming arms are always open. It poses no risks but offers instead a new kind of affluence, an embarrassment of riches so bountiful that material wealth simply pales by comparison.

But how can the modern woman—preoccupied with domestic tasks, marital and family relationships, a demanding career, and also frightened by a medical system that often seems to place pregnancy and childbirth in the realm of pathology—get in touch with the spiritual part of herself? And how can her partner accompany her on this journey? Like any journey to an uncharted destination, finding your spiritual center requires a new road map. Here are some ways to help you create that map.

   ❧ Imagine an ideal setting. It may be one that you have visited before, such as the beach or a ski chalet or a velvet-lined booth at the ballet. Or it may be an enchanting picture, even from your childhood, that depicted a sunny garden path, a cozy thatched cottage, and an arbor of tumbling roses.

    Once the picture is vivid and real to you, enter your ideal setting. Feel the sun's warmth on your face, see the snow-capped mountains, hear the orchestra's music, smell the roses.

    Remember this image, recall the beautiful feelings

it evokes in you, and consciously revisit it as often as possible.

❧ On an especially pretty piece of notepaper, write down your most cherished values. Is it family closeness, one of your God-given talents, your ability to give and receive love? How about that Dresden China doll from your girlhood? Yes, material possessions count; often they define us in unique and special ways.

Keep this list near at hand, add to it freely, and refer to it often, especially when problems threaten to eclipse your perspective. And think about pinning this uncommon inventory onto a bulletin board or hanging it on the refrigerator—after all, what is more important than your values?

❧ Think about (or write down) what you like or love most about your life. The chirping sounds of birds as you open your eyes in the morning? The challenge and excitement of your job? The warm hugs of your partner? As your spiritual awareness blossoms, you will find yourself adding to this list as well.

❧ Focus your attention on only one aspect of a particular task or object. If you're scrambling an egg, observe its liquid contents dropping from the shell into the bowl. Notice how the distinctly yellow and white parts of the egg become blended as you mix them vigorously with a fork. Watch as this blended liquid becomes increasingly solid and scrambled during its preparation. Note the egg's position on your plate in relation to the toast. See the palette that you have created with the saffron-colored egg, the strawberry jam, the tawny toast. Focusing precisely upon an event is a wonderful way to sharpen your senses, make yourself aware of the little miracles of everyday life, and enhance your spiritual awareness.

❧ Treat yourself as you would an honored guest. If you're eating alone, even just grabbing a bite, set the table as if it were for a feast—with a table setting and napkin, an attractive glass or cup, perhaps a vase of flowers or a brightly flickering candle. Attend to your surroundings so that they are as clean and pleasing as they would be for company. Whether at work or in a more casual setting, dress to feel pretty. These actions will add no more than a minute or two to your normal schedule, but all of them will heighten your pleasure and endow you with a greater appreciation of the important place you occupy in the universe.

❧ Make a written inventory of your life. Reflect on whether or not this is the life that you want to be leading. Are there areas that you would like to improve, enhance, or eliminate? In a "To be grateful for" column, enumerate your blessings, your strengths, your wishes and desires. In a "To work on" column, list problems that require solutions. By assessing your life in this way, you will be paying attention to the very central role that you play in your own life, in your relationship with your partner, and in the deep, lifelong spiritual bond that you will have with your child.

There is no one direct route to spiritual awareness. You may reach this destination through the side road of accidental discovery, the dirt path of adversity, the cloverleaf of hard-learned lessons, or the superhighway of blazing insight and wisdom. But however you seek your spiritual center, you will never hit a dead end. The spirit of life is all around you and richly within you, waiting for your embrace.

Chapter
Two

Creating a Spiritual Space
Random Moments of Richness

To begin your spiritual journey, a first good step is creating a spiritual space—a daily respite in which you enable the rays of spiritual sunshine that are all around to illuminate your life. This "space" can be a stretch of minutes or, even better, many random moments throughout the day.

Consider this. There are 168 hours in every week, which add up 10,080 minutes. If you sleep for 8 hours each night—which most women only dream of—that leaves 112 hours a week of wakefulness, or 6,720 minutes.

That's a lot of minutes, although it seems that none of us ever has enough time. But if you take 20 minutes a day from this total to enhance your spiritual awareness or, better, sprinkle your days with arbitrary moments of spiritual richness, you will be giving yourself a lifelong present.

This may not be quite as simple as first promised, any more than resolving to do "just 10 to 20 minutes" of exercise or even stealing 2 minutes to take a few deep breaths. In fact, anything we're not accustomed to is easy to promise but hard to bring about.

Yet, creating a spiritual space is far easier than revving yourself up to exercise or finding those 2 precious minutes. What is magical about such a space is its flexibility—it can be anywhere and anytime you want to make it. You can be driving your car, teaching a class, conducting business across your desk, trying a case in court, performing surgery, sitting at your kitchen table, nursing a patient, or taking a shower—yes, spiritual moments can enrich your life anywhere and anytime. Even in the middle of an argument.

Unfolding a Napkin

The secret to creating a spiritual space is in realizing that you don't have to block out anything. Unlike many forms of meditation that require you to clear your mind and focus on either a mantra or your inner sensations, creating a spiritual space involves opening up the mind and allowing new ideas to enter your consciousness.

Have you ever lain in your bed in the dark, fiddling with the radio dial to find your favorite station? All at once, you hear something wonderful. It might be a fascinating talk show or the lilt of some lovely piece of music. It's not your station, but it's so riveting that you stop fiddling and enjoy your new discovery.

Creating your spiritual space is exactly that—turning the dial of your mind until you happen upon a thought that you've rarely had before. More simply stated, it's "seeing" the things you have always known were there, but in a new way.

Consider the ancient Japanese meditation that is performed before meals. During this ritual the meditator concentrates on the simple act of unfolding a linen napkin. She reflects on her ability to feel the fabric's texture in her hands, to see the many subtle hues in its color, to smell its freshness, and to contemplate its uses. Slowly, deliberately, she concentrates on each sense and each sensation, appreciating as never before the many gifts and abilities this act requires.

She regards with wonder the complexity of her body's nervous system, endocrine system, brain, and heart, and the ways in which they collaborate to bring about the quite ordinary act of unfolding a napkin. She imagines what life would be like if her fingers were unable to work, if her eyes could not see, if the world of scents were denied to her, if any of the untold processes involved in this simple act were unavailable to her. And she thanks God for the awesome ability to unfold a napkin.

Yes, intellect and emotions play their part in this spiritual experience. But, like the beach visitor who comes to see that great, inexplicable forces are at work, the napkin unfolder elevates the uncomplicated process of unfolding a napkin to a higher plane. No longer is it an automatic act performed without thought or appreciation.

Rather, it becomes an opportunity to reflect on the gifts that God has given her. She feels humble and also grateful to be able to sit in silence, take up the neatly wrapped material before her, and unfurl it onto her lap. She has seen the unfolding in a new way, a way that enriches her life and makes not only this act but numerous other small deeds wondrous to her.

Like the napkin unfolder, you can experience even the mundane in new and remarkable ways. At first, opening up your consciousness to new ways of thinking may require discipline. But within just a few practice sessions, you will find yourself gravitating toward your new and uplifting way of thinking.

A good start is to unfold a napkin yourself. The secret

to deriving spiritual sustenance from such an exercise is to concentrate all of your attention on the task at hand. This wonderful exercise is followed, of course, by partaking of the meal for which the napkin will be used and by utilizing all of your senses in handling the dish, glass, fork, spoon, and knife.

Interestingly, many women instinctively gravitate toward this kind of active meditation during pregnancy, using their mysterious, womanly sensibilities to calm their minds and tap their spiritual centers. While unfolding a napkin may not be part of a woman's typical repertoire, the booties she knits, the afghan she fashions, the homey adages she cross-stitches, or the bib she embroiders all add to her serenity and to the joyous, maternal impulse to give her baby (even before birth) gifts of handcrafted and heartfelt love.

In this frenetic, mile-a-minute age, these traditional pursuits have been somewhat lost. But who better than you to reclaim them and, by so doing, establish this lovely spiritual union.

A Haven of Spirituality

Here's how to create your own haven of spirituality. Like the beach visitor and the napkin unfolder mentioned earlier, it will allow you to savor each moment that you are alive, transcend adverse situations, and become closer to God and the magnificent universe in which we live.

Open Up Your Senses

If you're in the midst of something that you've done for what seems like a million times before, for instance, getting a manicure, try to think not only of the outfit your nail polish color will match or the problems that have been preoccupying you that day but of the uplifting aspects of your surroundings.

See how the light from the window accents your manicurist's cheekbones. Imagine that you're an artist and not a lawyer (accountant, nurse, stockbroker). If you were painting a picture of the woman before you, how would you change her position to capture the essence of your picture? Take a moment to appreciate the fact that your eyes are able to see.

Feel the lotion that the manicurist applies to your skin and the movement of her hands as she massages your hands. How does it feel? Soothing? Harsh? Take a moment to appreciate that you are able to experience the sense of touch.

Hear the sounds around you. Is the music melodious, too loud, nonexistent? Pay attention to a sound that you may have blocked out before: a honking horn, a wailing siren, the chatter that surrounds you. Imagine for a moment how beautiful the memory of these would be if, all at once, you were deprived of your hearing. Take a moment to thank God that you can hear.

In all of these moments you will be sensing things that were always there but that you may not have taken the time to appreciate before. One of the amazing things about spiritual thinking is that, like a baby developing in the womb, it has a way of growing and blossoming, even outside your awareness.

Use Your Imagination

Imagine a new scenario for a meeting that may have been very stressful to you only a few hours before. Try to visualize the other people at the meeting, not as your coworkers but as extras on a film set or prison inmates or members of the Senate. This kind of imaginative thinking will give you perspective, allowing you to see yourself in the entire context of the world in which you live. Remind yourself that your meeting is one of millions of meetings going on in the world, all of whose members believe that their tasks are of monumental importance.

Now, picture a group of neurosurgeons peering at imaging scans and trying to decide how best to operate on a child's brain, or doctors trying to develop an ethics code for telling women that they have the breast cancer gene. Yes, our individual lives are important, but in the larger scheme of things—like the ocean, the sky, and a child's brain surgery—we are relatively small. Rather than being deflating or depressing, these ideas can be liberating. After all, why should we expect ourselves to be larger than the universe? Take a moment to thank God for giving you this sense of perspective. This is what spirituality is all about.

Concentrate on Little Things

I once met a woman named Rena, whose name in Hebrew means joy. But when Rena became pregnant at the age of 34, there was no joy in her life. Six months earlier, her mother had died, and Rena was still mourning her death. Rena was on the verge of gaining a much-coveted promotion in her high-powered career as a Wall Street broker but was feeling nervous and exhausted all the time. Although she and her husband had tried to conceive for four years, lately they had not been getting along, and her missed period came more as a shock than a welcome surprise.

When I saw Rena as a psychotherapy patient, she was depressed, ambivalent about having the baby, and worried about both her marriage and her ability to handle an even more demanding job. She mentioned to me that she had collected butterflies as a child but seemed annoyed when I suggested that she visit the butterfly exhibition in the Museum of Natural History. I asked her to tell me about butterfly wings. "I'm falling apart," she said, "and you want me to look at butterfly wings."

We spent the entire next session discussing butterfly wings. As she spoke, Rena became more and more energized, describing the differences between the colors and configurations of a monarch's and a viceroy's and an emperor's wings. I asked Rena how she had collected butterflies as a child, and she launched into a vivid description of taking trips into the woods, buying special kinds of nets, learning how to mount her specimens, overcoming the teasing of friends who called her The Moth Girl, and learning a complicated subject by sheer determination.

The next time I saw Rena, she smiled and said, "Now I know why you asked me to talk about butterflies instead of all the grief in my life. It took me back to my childhood and the excitement that I had felt as a collector. It showed me that when I put my mind to something, there's nothing I can't do. But most of all, I recaptured the miracle of it all."

It was not long before Rena was utilizing her newfound optimism in sharing what she called "the miracle of it all" with her husband. Rena did not consider herself particularly religious, but she had incorporated a spiritual dimension into her life, her relationship with her husband, and her new mother-to-be status that carried her through her pregnancy and birth with equanimity and peace.

Think Twice

This recommendation may seem to fly against the usual advice to be decisive. But in spite of the fact that most of us pay close attention to how we feel and go with our gut feelings, I have found that consciously thinking twice is a wonderful way to tap your spiritual center.

Let's go back to the child who is having brain surgery. Ordinarily, when we hear of such a calamity, we wince and express regret. "How terrible," we say, "how frightening." And then, because the mind can entertain only so many unsettling thoughts, we distance ourselves from the subject. This distancing can be one of our best defense mechanisms, a way to block out those things that weigh us down and that, for the most part, we can't do anything about. But the next time you hear of something upsetting, instead of retreating from it, try to think of it in a new way.

A few years ago, my mother had serious surgery. When she came home, I expected her to express the normal anxieties that most people feel after such surgery, such as nervousness about follow-up treatments and worry about the future. Instead, she was positively beaming.

When I told her it was wonderful to see her in such an upbeat mood, she said, "Why shouldn't I be? If it weren't for modern advertising, I might never have gone for that 'prevention' test. If I hadn't gone for the test, I might never have known about my condition. If I hadn't known about my condition, I would never have had the surgery. If modern medicine were not so advanced, there wouldn't have been surgery available to me. And if I hadn't had the surgery, the condition would have gotten worse and I wouldn't be sitting here now feeling so well."

My mother is no Pollyanna. She is worldly and erudite and has never deluded herself about life's realities. She knew the seriousness of her condition, but she had found—accurately—all of the positives in her experience. I attributed this to a life spent not only in dynamic pursuits but also in spiritual awareness.

She told me she had always questioned life's mysteries and had found all the answers in God's wisdom. "Every

*day is a gift," she said, "and every event, even a bad one,
gives me the opportunity to learn something I never
knew before." As a result, everything that life has
offered (or thrust upon) my mother has had a positive—
and very spiritual—dimension.*

What I'm suggesting is precisely the kind of thinking
that we hate when it's offered to us by others. What is
more irritating than complaining to a friend, only to have
her tell you that your particular grievance isn't so bad or
that there are children starving around the world? But it's
quite a different story when you yourself provide this perspective. From others, the advice may seem preachy or pa-
tronizing, but when you remind yourself to think about
any circumstance in a new way, you open up a world of
unimagined and rich possibilities.

Help

No, this is not a suggestion to seek help but rather to
give it. Often, especially when difficult life events threaten
to eclipse your perspective, it is natural to think that your
problems are too much to deal with. This is the perfect
time to do for others what you would like others to do for
you—help.

It could be something as simple as calling a long-lost
friend, volunteering 2 hours of your time at a nursing
home, or buying a gift for someone special in your life. By
getting outside yourself, you will enter a spiritual realm
and fulfill that most life-affirming Golden Rule: Do unto
others as you would have others do unto you.

Laugh

Does this seem to be a strange way to tap into your
spiritual nature? It is, in fact, a wonderful way. You may be

a person to whom laughter comes naturally. If so, you already know that life can be a very funny business, with all of what Shakespeare called our "strutting and fretting" upon the stage of life.

Perhaps this is why God made laughter so close to tears; they're both part of the same soup. When you laugh at a joke, chuckle at an idea, delight at the sight of something amusing, you are also acknowledging that, yes, this serious thing called life is also quite preposterous and full of mirth.

For some, this is the best route to perspective, to the acknowledgment that our most serious concerns must be weighed and measured against the next person's. If laughter does not come easily to you, then rent a hilarious video, buy a book of sidesplitting jokes, or spend an evening in a comedy club. Most good humor speaks of life itself, about what makes us human and vulnerable and also a part of a universe that is beyond our comprehension but that is fully comprehended by God. How comforting this is, that the deepest, most tear-inspiring belly laugh is, in fact, a spiritual act.

Drink in the Arts

Visit an art museum, attend a ballet, listen to a concert, buy a ticket to a musical show, or go to the movies. Over the centuries nothing has proved more affecting to the human spirit than the arts.

It is when engaging in or witnessing artistic pursuits that people become closer to both the mysterious and uplifting aspects of the spirit. Perhaps this is because the creation of art corresponds most closely to the richest of human experiences—the creation of a human life.

Music, in particular, invades one's spiritual center, and you can experience this virtually every day. When you're in your car, choose a cassette that moves you with its merry lilt, its lush romantic melody, its soaring crescendos, or its meaningful or uplifting lyrics.

If you're inspired to sing along, wonderful. If it makes you weep, those tears were in you to be shed. If it arouses anger or delight or sentimentality or inspiration, what a wonderful way to connect with your inner self. Of course, playing the radio or compact disc player, taking up an instrument you may have put away, or simply humming to yourself are other ways to fill your spiritual life with music.

Learn from Nature

A great route to spiritual insight comes from observing the world around you. By simply observing butterfly wings, Rena was able to see her own life in perspective and translate her newfound vision in life-affirming ways. Concentrate on an ant colony, watch a buzzing bee hover over a flower, spend some time at the zoo, marvel at the lush flower that has emerged from a tiny seed, gaze at a flock of birds in flight, or open an oyster for its pearl. Soon, you will be acquiring pearls of wisdom, of insight, and of spiritual enlightenment. Every lesson in the world, everything that we mortals can comprehend, can be learned from nature.

Finding a Spot of One's Own

It is almost impossible to measure the delirious joy of treasure hunters who spend years searching the depths of the ocean or the interiors of remote grottos and finally come upon a trove of glinting jewels, ancient coins, or crowns and scepters. But their joy pales in comparison to the exhilaration of the person who happens upon her spiritual center. The deep elation, the sense of harmony and peace, and the insight and wisdom that such a discovery brings is truly incalculable.

But like treasure hunters, seekers of spiritual bliss must also dig deep, within themselves and outside themselves, in the enigmatic design of nature. Often, this search requires solitude, a place where thinking and feeling are uncluttered by the distractions of everyday life. For every woman who is contemplating pregnancy or already pregnant, such a place is equal to or even greater in importance than nutrition and rest.

But where to find such a place? When you're home alone, take a leisurely stroll throughout the interior and exterior of your residence. Observe your surroundings in a new way, contemplating an empty alcove, an unutilized space, a quiet corner on the porch, a storeroom, a window with a lovely view. In your imagination, rope off this spot and add to it enhancing features, such as a favorite picture, a philodendron, a pretty bottle, or a strand of pearls.

Now, picture yourself occupying this spot, sitting contentedly alone with your thoughts and feelings. This can be your daily getaway, a place where you can spend 10 to 20 minutes in spiritual contemplation and inward reflection.

"Impossible," you may say. But not if you explain to your partner the importance of such a respite and ask his assistance in making sure that phone calls, doorbells, and other interruptions don't intrude on the special quiet time that you have forged for yourself.

Try God

When I say "Try God," I mean that in the most literal sense. Try believing in something larger, wiser, more powerful than yourself. This is not to suggest that you abandon your personality, your brains, your ambitions, your fantasies, your vulnerabilities, your anything to God—quite the contrary. It is to tell you that God loves you as you are and that this love is so powerful and all-embracing that it will be your ally and your protector for all time.

When Things Go Wrong

Will God's love protect you against adversity? Illness? Pain and heartbreak? No. These are all parts of the human condition—a state that distinguishes mere mortals as, well, mere mortals. Think about the woman who has embarked on her parenting voyage full of hope and optimistic anticipation, only to experience a personal tragedy, an illness, a premature delivery, or the birth of a child with overwhelming problems. When the natural order of things goes awry in this way, it is also natural to question the existence of a merciful or omniscient God and to rage against the cruelty of fate.

Johanna had waited for eight years to marry Bill while she cared for her ailing parents. During their lengthy relationship, their strong faith in God's wisdom sustained them, and they spent untold hours fantasizing about the day when they would be able to spend their lives together. "Our number one fantasy," she told me, "was a big family."

When Johanna was 35 and Bill a few years older, they finally married. "We didn't waste one second," Johanna said. "After only two months, I was pregnant and we danced around the kitchen like teenagers at a prom." It would be years before Johanna would dance again.

Like the biblical Job, a torrent of tragedies befell Johanna. In her third month, Bill was killed in a car accident. In her fifth month, while in deep mourning, she discovered a tumor that required immediate surgery. Suffering with anxiety over the risks that general anesthesia posed to her baby, she underwent the operation and was relieved, to say the least, that the tumor was benign.

But at the end of her seventh month, she went into

premature labor and delivered her beloved son, Billy, who required life-saving measures and more than six weeks of hospitalization. As Billy got older, he had a variety of learning problems and trouble with his eyes.

"I hated God," Johanna said. "After everything that had happened, all I could do was cry all day. I thought I had done everything right, and I found myself walking around my house screaming, 'How could you do this to me? You're a fake.' All my life I believed that God was kind. But where was the kindness?"

Johanna would be the first to agree that God works in mysterious ways. Six years after Billy's birth, she was flourishing. "Except for Bill's tragic death," she told me, "I'm the luckiest person in the world." She said that little Billy's problems had opened up a whole world that she had never known about before.

Fueled by her own traumatic experiences and the demands of a child with various difficulties, she had completed her degree in social work, become deeply involved in fighting for legislation for children with learning disabilities, and initiated a bereavement group for widows and widowers—at which she met her future husband.

"A couple of years after Billy was born," she said, "I was looking for direction. I was still depressed, but I knew that I needed help, so I reluctantly turned back to God. And when I did, he was right there. I had left him, but he had never left me. I don't wish what happened to me on anyone, but whenever I meet someone who has been through tragedy, I know that something meaningful and wonderful can come out of that tragedy. That is just how God works. I'm a different person now, a better person, and I hope wiser, too."

Does Johanna's insight, "This is how God works," sound too simple? We are so accustomed to thinking that complex problems require complex solutions that we often miss the rich smorgasbord of choices and possibilities that lie before us in plain view or the simple answers that faith itself provides.

We may not understand how God works, but we don't have to. When you tap into your spiritual nature, you will find God and God will let you know that you are exactly who you should be—or can be—and that whoever you are, a nonjudgmental, loving presence is with you and will be with you through conception and labor and birth, through joy and through adversity.

So there you have it, guidelines to help you find your spiritual center. Now, let's consider the preamble to having a baby—those twinkles in your eyes, the lovemaking, and the ways in which you and your partner can share a spiritual space that will bring you closer to each other, to your baby, and to God.

Chapter
Three

Contemplating Pregnancy

From a Twinkle in the Eye
to Making Love

Whether a pregnancy is planned or accidental, the creation of a baby is life's most profound experience. If planned, however, long, hard thought will go into weighing and measuring the many considerations that this life-changing event will entail. Is this the best time to get pregnant? Will it affect my marriage? My love life? My job? My lifestyle? Can I support a baby financially? What kind of mother will I be? If I continue working, who will care for my baby?

Thinking We, Not Me

The decision to have a baby often requires a reassessment not only of your career but also of your value system, your roles—in short, your whole life. Today, many couples marry and become parents for the first time after the age of 30. Before then, each of them may not have been called upon to think about, worry about, take care of, or sacrifice for anyone else but themselves.

After having lived a full three or more decades, part of that time independently, it is not always easy for couples to envision making room for a dependent human being who will need them (or a caring surrogate) every minute of every day—for years. Marriage or living together may present a segue to this challenge, since sharing one's life with another person demands thought, worry, care, and sometimes sacrifice, but parenthood is a whole new kettle of fish.

One way to avoid, or at least minimize, future problems is to think—before pregnancy takes place—about the ways in which parenthood will change your lives. It is not enough to tackle these issues on an intellectual level; rational thought is not the greatest route to emotional insight. Looking at them solely from an emotional point of view is not sufficient either; before your baby is born, you definitely feel that the baby will have the highest priority.

But including a spiritual perspective in your decision is bound to yield a greater appreciation of the relative importance of things and how you and your baby will fit into the universe. It will allow you to review and perhaps reassess your value system and to contemplate the influence that you will have in shaping your baby's life.

That is not to say that your best intentions will result in a perfect outcome. If good intentions determined how the events of our lives turned out, we would all live in a pretty perfect world. All of us know caring parents whose children resented them, just as we know of neglectful parents whose children honored them. A child whose father is drafted into war may feel abandoned or proud. A child whose mother suffers from an illness may feel ignored or sympathetic.

The vagaries of the human heart and the unpredictability of subjective interpretation are incomprehensible, but that should not inspire parents-to-be to embrace a roll-of-the-dice view of life. By and large, the thought, worry, care, and especially sacrifice of parents are what parenting is all about, so a me-first attitude is not the best way to set the stage for this important event.

A helpful way to think about this serious subject is to ask yourself questions about how life might be after your baby is born. If your child were to get sick, how would that affect your work life? If you couldn't find a baby-sitter, would you resent having to stay home? How would you feel about sacrificing a vacation in order to be able to pay for music lessons or braces or a tutor? Who will get up in the middle of the night? Who will forgo a business appointment? How will you teach your child values and what will those values be?

Asking and answering these questions honestly will give you a penetrating look into your own psyche and tell you more about your relationship to the material world than any intellectual discussions will ever do. And they will allow you—again, before your baby is born—to evaluate and reevaluate your priorities.

If these issues have been on your mind, then you've already started to exhibit that twinkle in your eyes, that glittering sign of something quite thrilling in your future together. But a twinkle is just part of the process of making a baby. Just as cooking a delicious dinner or performing excellently at your job requires the right ingredients, an even more special combination of elements goes into the creation of the very unique life that you and your partner will present to the world.

This creation will require more thought and effort and expense than you have put into acquiring an education, buying a home or a car, or even gaining employment, all of which involve life's most momentous decisions. But these are all negotiable, nonbinding, potentially change-able, and, in the larger scheme of things, intrinsically transitory.

Educations are cut short, people move from their homes, cars are traded in, and careers—especially today, when life spans have increased significantly—change routinely, in some instances three or four times in a life-time. But parenthood is a constant. It's nonnegotiable and forever. How does one prepare for such a momen-tous event?

Tending to Your Physical Health

Your physical health is of primary importance. Well be-fore she conceives, a woman should already be eating a healthy, balanced diet. This is the ideal time to invest in a few visits with a nutritionist who is familiar with the spe-cial dietary needs of pregnancy and pre-pregnancy. Preg-nancy and birth will cost you many thousands of dollars; the relatively minimal expense of a nutritionist will be well worth some of them.

Boilerplate pregnancy diets won't always tell you every-thing. Some vitamins, for instance, can be harmful to the developing baby, and processed meats, caffeine, and high-sugar foods provide no nutrition at all. Allergies or pre-existing medical conditions may also require special dietary considerations as well as careful monitoring. And not all medications are safe, so all medications must be discussed in depth with your doctor.

This is also the time to swear off cigarettes and al-cohol completely and to establish a doable exercise rou-tine. If you've never been a physical-fitness buff, then this is the time to start that morning walk or that after-noon swim or build up to 30 minutes in the evening on a stationary bike.

Physical exercise, like music, is often a direct route to spiritual enlightenment. Out in the fresh air, away from life's hectic pace, your exertion will fuel those good-mood chemicals in your brain, bringing about a clarity of mind that will allow you to think twice about troublesome issues, to see your life in perspective, and to drink in the spirit of the universe. Even indoor exercise provides the same effect.

It is also time to learn if your job poses potential risks to the baby that you are—or soon hope to be—carrying. If the questions that you ask your employer do not yield satisfactory answers, don't hesitate to contact the Occupational Safety and Health Administration.

We now know that a baby's health no longer depends solely on the health of its mother. Several studies point to the negative effects of a father's alcohol or drug use on a child's development before birth. Alcohol depresses sperm production and potency as well as contributes to miscarriages. We also know that many types of illnesses can negatively affect the fragile embryo, particularly in the early months of development. So before thinking about conceiving, both mother and father should have physical checkups to assure that they are in good shape.

But you know all this. Thinking about it spiritually, as a woman named Celeste did, can bring a whole new dimension to the subject of physical well-being during pregnancy.

> *Celeste, a young, unmarried registered nurse and midwife, brought to her job both enthusiasm and commitment. "I loved helping to bring babies into the world," she said, "and spending time with new mothers, teaching them everything about health and nutrition and what their labors and deliveries would be like." She spent a great deal of time studying all the new theories and methods, she said, and, after several years, believed*

she was giving her patients the best prenatal care.

During one of her rare vacations, she and a friend decided to visit England. "I loved old castles," she bubbled. When she caught sight of her first castle, she said, "It took my breath away." She described the ancient structure's exterior as resplendent and inviting and said that she and her friend raced across the expansive lawns and made their way carefully over the moat to reach the imposing, 12-foot-high wooden doors.

"When we went in, the rooms were filled with multicolored tapestries, crystal chandeliers, burgundy brocades, and frescoed ceilings. There was history in every corner." But after a little while, Celeste's view of the castle changed. "Most of the windows were broken and they kept clanking," she said. "We had only brought a snack, so pretty soon we were starving, and even though the weather was nice outside, every room in that castle was freezing."

Snug in her hotel room that evening, Celeste fell into a deep sleep. At about three o'clock in the morning, she suddenly sat straight up in bed with a piercing insight. "I had a dream," she said.

"It wasn't me in the castle, it was a baby. But the castle wasn't the castle, it was a womb. And even though it looked beautiful on the outside and, at first, beautiful on the inside, it wasn't beautiful at all. It was noisy, and the baby was hungry, and it was freezing. And I knew that that's how it is for a lot of babies. All they hear in the womb is their parents screaming, and all they get is the same poor diet that their mothers have always gotten, and all they 'feel' is coldness because they're not in a nurturing environment."

Celeste's dream changed her profoundly. After her experience, whenever she taught her patients about the importance of health and nutrition, she told them of her dream. And the dream, she said, changed them, too.

Tending to Your Mental Health

Mental health is equally as important as physical well-being. We know the great toll that stress and depression take on fully grown adults. Both common sense and persuasive scientific studies indicate that the stresses that course through a woman's system, just as the foods she eats, have an effect on the fragile embryo who takes in whatever its mother takes in.

It's not a good idea to make any major decisions when you're depressed or anxious or "not yourself." If you have been feeling sad or nervous or having problems in your marriage, and you think that having a baby will change these things—that's truly not the case. Pregnancy requires many major physical and psychological adjustments, and parenthood necessitates even more. If possible, it's best to resolve as many problems as possible, especially those in your relationship with your partner.

Being in good physical and mental shape, however, are not the only criteria for planning a child. It's generally true that being in good financial shape bodes well for the growing family as well, so now is the time to analyze all contingencies.

What's in a Gene?

It is a good idea to avail yourself of what modern science now offers: genetic counseling. Genetic counselors offer an analysis of your family histories and physical tests that may warn you of any problems that your child can (or probably will) inherit. Genetic testing is indicated if a woman has had multiple miscarriages, if she has previously delivered a child with birth defects, if either parent belongs to an ethnic group at high risk for specific genetic diseases or has a relative with birth defects, if a woman has been exposed to high doses of radiation, or if she is over the age of 35.

While this kind of testing may appear frightening, it can also be viewed in a more positive way—as an opportunity to rethink the decision to become the biological parents of a child. If the mother's history is problem-free but her partner's is problematic, she may decide to opt for in vitro or artificial insemination, in which sperm is donated by another male (either of one's choosing or from an anonymous donor whose health history is known). A difficult decision, it is one that requires the greatest amount of spiritual and philosophical harmony between a woman and her partner.

> Nicole and Guy, both high-powered professionals— she, an architect; he, a state senator—faced this decision. Married while in college, they had deferred even thinking about having a baby until both were over 35 and flying high in their chosen fields. When they finally decided to become parents, "nothing happened," Nicole said. After a year, they went for testing and learned that Guy was sterile, apparently from a childhood case of the mumps.
>
> At first, they were both devastated, having fantasized for years about the qualities that their baby would inherit from each of them. "Nicole mentioned adoption or in vitro, but I had the attitude that my child had to have my genes," Guy said. "Anything else was out of the question. If I was going to have a child, I wanted to know what I was getting." As they debated the issue, their once-loving relationship became decidedly strained.
>
> Then, with what Guy called prophetic timing, he received a letter from a constituent, begging him to place wheelchair ramps in a town in one of the districts he represented. He invited the letter writer to visit his of-

fice so that he could learn more about the need for such ramps. The following week, two young children in wheelchairs arrived, followed by their mother, a warm and lively woman who stated her case simply.

"These are my terrific kids," she said of her eight-year-old, identical twin boys. "They were both born with spina bifida, but that's the only thing holding them back—that and the fact that they can't get everywhere they want to go because our town has no ramps." Before he could say anything, one of the twins piped up, "We just want to be independent."

Before going home that evening, Guy went to church to ask God's forgiveness. "I must be crazy," he said to God, "for thinking that my little disappointment means anything." He prayed for wisdom to accept and love and, if need be, fight for any child that he might be getting. When he got home, he told Nicole that he wanted her to try in vitro. Nicole was ecstatic.

In a somewhat unusual twist, they agreed to approach a colleague of Nicole's to be the donor, and he said yes—with no strings. The result was Dana, an incredible child who, ironically, looks like Guy.

If you find yourself in the same position as Nicole and Guy, you may choose to ask a friend to be the donor. But, in deciding to become a parent, Guy's revelation can serve as a guide. No couple can consult a crystal ball, and they all take the chance of not having a so-called perfect child.

Couples who face this possibility in a conscious, evolved way are better prepared to deal with the complex emotional and financial costs of raising a child who has problems. Many opt for the challenge; for others, like the mothers of Billy and the twins, the challenge simply happens. In any case, genetic testing is a good idea for anyone over the age of 35 contemplating parenthood. But no matter what age you are when you decide to become a parent or when you find yourself pregnant, other questions will absorb your attention.

Sharing the Riches

Parenting, as Nicole and Guy learned, is certainly the ultimate of life's joint ventures. Every facet of this venture can be immeasurably enriched by sharing all of its aspects, including the spiritual, with your partner. So when you are unfolding that napkin, opening up your senses, using your imagination, concentrating on little things, laughing, trying God, or any of the other exercises that will bring you closer to your spiritual center, share them.

Many of these activities are intrinsically solitary, yet speaking about them, exchanging ideas, or describing your subjective experiences will allow you and your partner to share the spiritual realm of bringing a new life into the world. And that is not to omit the many spiritual experiences you can have together—taking a nature walk, listening to a symphony, spending a morning in silence, communicating solely through touch, or just sitting with one another in quiet, loving togetherness.

The richness of these times together, the insights they will yield, and the strength they will give you to deal with whatever life has to present will enable both of you to face the future with optimism, resolve, and resilience.

Chapter
Four

Artists of the Masterpiece
The Expectant Parents

What are you to do if the blessings of physical or emotional well-being are not present in your life when you get pregnant? What if you're suffering from some physical condition or you're feeling depressed or you're having trouble with your partner or you've just lost your job or, especially, you've been through genetic testing and the results are iffy—or downright scary?

These circumstances are not uncommon. And that is why it's also important to be in good spiritual shape. Whatever the circumstances of your life, even if they're significantly less than optimal, spirituality can influence them most positively. I know a couple in their early thirties who discovered this when everything seemed to go wrong.

"My Eyes Opened Up"

Kara and Edgar were planning to have a baby when they were assailed by tough times. "We were blindsided," Kara said. When they decided to have a baby, they had been married for five years and had worked at their jobs since both were just out of graduate school. "Both of us had great jobs, nonstop jobs," Edgar said, "so it never seemed to be the right time to have a baby. But all of a sudden, Kara was 33 and I was 37, and we realized that it was probably now or never."

Kara was a legislative aide to a U.S. congressman, in charge of health issues. Edgar was an FBI agent, assigned to the office of the vice president. Their life in Washington was a whirlwind of excitement, gossip, and important activity, and they both loved what they were doing. After discussing every contingency and deciding that with the right planning they could continue working, they decided to go ahead and have a baby.

"Then everything fell apart," Kara said. "After 18 years in office, my boss lost his election, and I was out of a job. Edgar came back from a trip overseas with a strange bug that made him sick for so long that he had to take a protracted leave of absence. And both of us were depressed." The one thing that they managed to do on a regular basis was go to church. "I had no place else to go," Kara said, "and Edgar only had enough energy to go out for an hour, so that's where we ended up."

Kara admitted that both she and Edgar went to church out of habit. They weren't pagans, she explained, "but in Washington, church can become a social thing, even an image thing." They were so used to going to church for "the wrong reasons," she added, that "for the most part, we just sat there, except when we asked God, rather angrily, why so many bad things had happened to us."

One day, however, "My eyes opened up," Kara said. She was sitting in a pew with Edgar positioned uncomfortably at her side, when she noticed in a new way a statue of Mary. "Even before I took catechism in grade school," she said, "I knew that Jesus had died for my sins and that God loved me and that the Virgin Mary was loved by everyone. But all of a sudden, I saw Mary for the first time. There she was, holding her beloved son, looking at him with love—but he was dead. Dead! What did she feel like? I had lost my job, not a son. Edgar was sick, not dead."

Kara's blazing insight changed her life. "I said to Edgar, 'We're lucky, we're so lucky, and now is the time to have a baby. I knew that I'd get another job and that Edgar would feel better. Thank God, I made that decision." Less than a year later, Kara and Edgar thanked God again when their little Bernadette was born. By that time, Kara was back at work and Edgar was fully recovered, just as Kara had predicted.

This story demonstrates why it makes good sense to expend your most evolved talents, intelligence, and spiritual energies in planning to have a baby. Yet, thinking about the issue in a more mundane way also makes sense. Think about the last big project that you undertook, a business venture or even a party. Certainly, you worked hard, no doubt making your home spotless, planning a terrific menu, shopping carefully for the food, and preparing it with care.

You probably sent out beautiful, precisely written invitations. You may have even selected a particularly appropriate stamp to place on the envelope. And, of course, you made sure to select a wonderful outfit and paid great attention to all of its accoutrements. And let's not forget your hair, your nails, and the scent you chose. All this for a 3- to 4-hour party.

A Joint Venture

Getting into good spiritual shape is a little more elusive than going for a checkup or evaluating your mood. It starts with the artists who will create their masterpiece, the mom- and dad-to-be. With friends and family, you can joke about the subject. "We're thinking about it," you may say to those who ask if you're planning to have a baby.

But when you're in each other's company, first and foremost consider that this is the most important joint venture of your lives, one that deserves to be considered not in a passing conversation but when both of you are relaxed and have the time to discuss the subject in all of its breadth and depth. Now is the time for both of you to establish that inviolable spiritual space in which you can be alone together with your thoughts, your dreams, your contemplations, and your prayers.

Alone Together to Speak about Parenthood

If you can't seem to find that time, then make a date to be together away from the hustle and bustle of your normal lives. Go to a park and sit on a bench, look at the trees (and the swings and slides), and talk about what this baby will mean to you. Go to the beach, take a walk, drive in the country. Make a space to give this subject the importance that it deserves.

A wonderful exercise can help you get to the core of your feelings about having a baby and becoming a parent. First, the mom-to-be faces her partner and speaks about the subject for 5 minutes, with absolutely no interruption. During her monologue, she uses only the pronouns *I* and *me,* as her partner sits and listens. For instance:

"When I was thinking about getting pregnant, at first it made me very excited. I pictured myself holding the baby and everyone oohing and aahing. He would have my hair and his daddy's dimple, and would grow up in a wonderful world. But then I thought about the things that I've tried with no success or the projects I've lost interest in and it made me scared to think that this may happen with a baby. I remember when I was a little girl..."

She talks about her dreams, her fantasies, her fears. And, while she speaks, her partner is learning things that he may never have known about her and understanding her in new ways. He gains insight into the ways a pregnancy may affect her, and he feels closer to her than ever before. Then, it's his turn.

"I always thought that I would be the kind of father my father was. But that was in a different day and age. My dad went to work every day and my mom stayed home, and that was the way it was. I know I'll be more involved than he was as far as pitching in is concerned, but sometimes I worry that it will take away from my career and that I won't be there as much as I'm expected to be, and that our marriage may suffer."

He, too, speaks about his dreams, fantasies, and fears. While he speaks, his partner hears things she has never heard before and gets to understand him in a whole new way.

When both are finished speaking, they can discuss the issues that have arisen, approaching them nonjudgmentally and with empathy. This simple exercise, open and noncritical, establishes the fertile ground on which good relationships are based, and the happy parenting that derives from such relationships.

But before you do this exercise again, take a few days in between to digest what you have discussed. Emotional revelations can be startling, both to ourselves and to those who are closest to us. I know that we live in a unisex age in which many people strive to minimize the gender issues that have always divided men and women and to equalize male and female experiences—but that is theory. By and large, women are still more comfortable expressing emotion, so they may be more ready to resume this kind of exchange the next day, while some men may need a little more time.

A pretty reliable rule is to do what musicians in a band do when they haven't received the sheet music and, therefore, are not sure of the tune that they're supposed to be playing: "When in doubt, lay out." In other words, don't push the subject until both of you have had time to really think about what you have shared with each other. Then, you will be more than ready to have another mom- and dad-to-be session.

As you learn more about each other from these self-disclosing exchanges, conflicts may arise. "I somehow thought you'd want to stay home with the baby—at least for six months," the man may say. "I can't believe you want our child to go to military school," the woman may say. How wonderful that you are discussing these issues before they cause havoc at a later date. By getting them out in the open, you are halfway to solving them, or at least to finding a compromise.

Other issues will arise as well: which doctor or midwife you will choose, the pediatrician you will select, the logistics of child care, the decision of whether to breast-feed or bottle-feed, the help you will give each other after the baby is born, the kind of home you want to establish, the religion you will practice, the values you share and want to impart, the ways you will spend money.

Of course, as life evolves and you evolve with it, things

may change—that is the nature of life. At this point, how-ever, the more you are in harmony, the more issues you have brought out in the open and resolved, the better your baby's beginning will be.

Seeing Your Baby-to-Be in Other Children

As you begin to speak about having your own baby, you may find yourself noticing as you never have before little children playing in a sandbox or climbing on a jungle gym or pedaling their tricycles. As you watch these seemingly ordinary activities, as you hear the shrieks of joy and the cries of frustration, you will marvel at the ability of these little ones to see, speak, hear, skip, jump, and run.

You will realize that it takes more than physical and mental health and taking the right vitamins to bring forth such a perfect being. What an ideal time to pray that your child will be blessed with these gifts, and you will trust in the towering wisdom of a God who knows more than mere mortals how the universe works.

You will also trust that the strength of your relationship and the spiritual bond that you have established with each other will give you the fortitude and wisdom and love to deal with a child who may lack all of the extraordinary gifts that you now appreciate as never before.

Creating a Journal

This is a perfect time to begin a personal journal, to start to record the many thoughts, dreams, fantasies, and fears that have started to capture your imagination or haunt your waking hours. Here are some guidelines for your journal.

Be Honest

Contemplating parenthood often arouses a mixture of feelings, everything from joy to anxiety, from excitement to fear. Write down everything. Don't be inhibited. The very act of recording your emotions will be liberating, and your chronicle will allow you to chart the course of your feelings and to reflect on them as the days and weeks and months elapse. Often, initial anxieties become minor or nonexistent concerns over time.

> In the early months of her pregnancy, Janice became obsessed with the fear that sleeping on her stomach would smother her baby. So fearful was she that, instead of getting the rest she needed, she became an insomniac. "Sometimes, I would stay up all night," she said, "trying to make sure that I was sleeping on my back and not turning over."
>
> When a friend suggested that she write down her fears, Janice found herself scrawling pages and pages of long-suppressed memories of being at sleep-away camp when she was nine and hearing the plaintive yowls of a wild raccoon outside her bunk. "When we woke up the next morning, the raccoon was lying dead, with her little baby raccoons dead by her side," she recalled. "I remember the counselor saying, 'Her belly couldn't take it,' and in my mind I somehow thought she had smothered them." By writing down these buried thoughts, Janice realized that her perceptions when she was nine years old were just that—perceptions of a nine-year-old.
>
> "I must have written 15 pages about this incident," Janice said. "But after I had put it all down and relived the horror of that experience, I was over it—just like that. I slept the best night's sleep I had had in months."

Janice confided her anxiety to her husband, Kevin. At first, he was bewildered, even frightened. But when Janice showed him her writing and they discussed her camp experience, he was extremely supportive, helping her to gain insight into, and finally overcome, her fear. Another woman, Wendy, kept her anxiety to herself.

When Wendy came to my Lamaze class, she was seven months pregnant. Accompanied by her attentive and loving husband, Justin, she initially appeared content with her life. After the last class, she called me, weeping so uncontrollably that she could hardly get her words out.

"I have the perfect life," she sobbed, "a beautiful home, a loving husband, a beautiful little boy. But since the second that I knew I was pregnant, all I could think about was having a girl, and I just know that if I don't have a daughter, I'll have a nervous breakdown."

Wendy told me that she thought about this every minute of every day. "No matter how happy I look to other people," she said, "I feel torn up inside. I've never been more miserable in my life." I recommended a therapist to Wendy and asked her to stay in touch with me.

Three months later, Wendy called. "I'd like to visit," she said. "I want to show off my new baby." When she carried her new little son into my living room, she was beaming. She told me that through therapy, she had learned how being a lifelong perfectionist had made her feel that she had to present an ideal picture to the world. The oldest of three children, she had two younger brothers, one of whom had physical problems, the other of whom had emotional problems. "I was the star in my family," she explained, "the one who was supposed to make my parents happy and do everything right."

When Wendy's mother told her how perfect it would be if her second child were a girl, Wendy interpreted her remarks not as a wish but as a directive. As a result, she had spent almost her entire pregnancy in a state of anxiety and depression. Fortunately, she was so determined

to resolve her problem that she saw the therapist three
times a week in her ninth month, and for several
months after she delivered.

Wendy's story demonstrates the importance of not keeping your anxieties bottled up inside. Fears and anxieties are common during pregnancy. In fact, sometimes powerful emotions that have long been kept in check surface at this time.

A good rule for dealing with troublesome thoughts or feelings is to tell yourself, "If I am having them, they are normal." And they are—maybe disturbing, maybe scary, maybe perplexing. But normal in the sense that the human mind typically entertains every imaginable kind of thought, good and bad. So, share your anxieties with trusted people and, if necessary, don't hesitate to seek professional help.

Analyze Your Dreams

When women are contemplating pregnancy, and when they are pregnant, their dreams often become more vivid than ever. Freud said that dreaming is our way of "going crazy" safely, of expressing our unconscious feelings without experiencing the fear that they may evoke if we thought the same things in a fully conscious way.

It is not uncommon for pregnant women to dream about going on long trips to foreign lands, about looking into a mirror and not recognizing themselves, about falling from a great height or scaling a great mountain, even about killing. If you are a particularly vivid dreamer, you may want to keep a separate dream journal. When you are looking back on this time of your life, you will be fascinated by this written record.

When Larissa became my psychotherapy patient, she
was in the sixth month of a pregnancy that she

described as "no problem." Except, she said, for a recurrent dream in which she was being pursued by unknown assailants from whom she tried desperately to escape. As her dream progressed, they caught up to her and began to bind her to a post with wide bands of burlap material. She struggled to unshackle herself and almost succeeded, but just when she was breaking free, her aggressors lashed her head to the post and covered her eyes and mouth. She always awoke from this dream gasping for breath, in a heart-thumping panic.

Larissa immediately related the dream to her past and current life and to the conscious anxiety she had about becoming a mother. The daughter of two parents who were deaf, she had grown up speaking several languages: sign language, English, and the Polish she had learned from her grandmother, who lived with the family.

"I guess I always wondered why I could hear and my parents couldn't," she said, "and even when I was a little girl, I thought about the possibility of having children who couldn't hear." As she got older, Larissa realized that she had a gift for language and decided to become an interpreter. By the time she finished graduate school, she spoke fluent Italian, French, Portuguese, and German, and, to her delight, became one of the youngest interpreters at the United Nations.

After several months of trying to figure out her dream, she came to my office grinning from ear to ear. "I got it," she announced. "My assailants—that's my fear that something bad will happen to me or my baby. Tying me to the post—that's my fear that I won't have any power. The burlap, I don't know what that is, but covering my eyes—that's because I wasn't seeing what my problem was. But covering my mouth, that's the most important part of the dream because that is what my strength has always been—speaking, interpreting, understanding."

Larissa's comprehension of her recurrent dream ended it. Again, she had become an interpreter, only this time she had deciphered the language of the unconscious. You can interpret your dreams as well. By discussing them, relating them to your past or current life, and using the symbolism of which dreams are made to decode their messages, you can learn this fascinating language and, at the same time, gain insight into your own fascinating psyche.

Indulge Your Fantasies

For some people fantasy comes naturally. Even those who live perfectly conventional lives may have rich fantasy lives in which they routinely picture themselves in exotic places, among extraordinary people, engaged in fantastic exploits. Fantasies, by definition, are departures from what we commonly recognize as reality. They are the products of imagination—our dreams, visions, and illusions.

For the most part, fantasies are pleasurable, allowing us to escape into a rich world of treasured wishes and cherished dreams. Who has not sat in immovable traffic, imagining the comforts of home? Who has not bought a lottery ticket and fantasized about the life of wealth and ease that this windfall would bring? What woman has carried a baby and not had visions of a beautiful cherub nestling blissfully in her arms? Yes, fantasies allow us to dream impossible dreams and even envision their actualization.

At the same time, fantasies—when not recognized for their ephemeral and illusive nature—can set people up for disappointment.

> *Lonica said that she had dreamed about becoming a mother since she got her first life-size Mama Doll at the age of four. "I was a natural mother, even then," she said. A willowy young woman with upswept black hair*

and a distinctly Victorian air, she told me that she had talked about having babies on her first date with Evan, the man who became her husband.

"Even before I got pregnant," she chirped, "I was em-broidering coverlets for my baby, looking at antique wooden cradles, collecting silver spoons and cups, and sewing glorious maternity clothes. I knew this would be the most wonderful event in my life."

When she became pregnant shortly after her marriage, Lonica's fantasies became even more expansive. She and Evan had bought a small cottage with, yes, a white picket fence, and bowers of flowers covered the trellises that framed what she called their heavenly home. She told me that she pictured herself wearing long, flowing dresses, greeting Evan each evening with frosted glasses of iced tea topped with spearmint sprigs, and surrounding herself with beautiful music, skeins of yarn, and books of spiritual enlightenment.

From the first week of her pregnancy, however, Lonica suffered from nausea and vomiting. When she noticed a few spots of blood, her doctor recommended bed rest. Her breasts felt sore all the time, and her only activity seemed to be going to the bathroom to urinate. "I couldn't even get out of my nightgown," she said. "The thought of iced tea made me sick. The sound of music made me sick. Looking at my knitting needles made me throw up. And when I thought about reading, I would get a wave of nausea. Everything I had imag-ined had no reality."

Lonica was devastated by the disparity between her fantasy of pregnancy and its uncomfortable reality. By her fourth month, her nausea had abated, but she still felt depressed. "It was the first time I understood what shattered dreams meant," she lamented. "It was also the first time I knew that I had grown up."

By her fifth month, Lonica had regained her optimism and was able to fulfill many of her fantasies. She had learned to recognize the dreamlike nature of her fantasy life and to reconcile it with the reality of life itself. Like Wendy, who could only imagine having a daughter, Lonica had become so immersed in her fantasies about pregnancy that the intrusion of reality was crushing. Fortunately, both of their experiences had a happy ending. Wendy was helped through psychotherapy, and Lonica was helped by a supportive husband and simply by the passage of time.

Fantasy life is an intrinsic part of pregnancy. Whether your fantasies are idyllic or disturbing, share them. Expressing your hopes and dreams or your doubts and nightmares to your partner will bring you closer together. And, because men are usually more reluctant to indulge in fantasies (at least verbally), your willingness to share your fantasies may be the key that unlocks your partner's inhibitions.

"Birds Do It, Bees Do It . . ."

Keeping a journal, discussing your dreams or anxieties with your partner, and engaging in deep, intimate talk with him about having a baby—all are a wonderful preamble to the momentous task of creating a baby. But, as we all know, it takes more than philosophical contemplations and talk to bring a baby into the world. In Cole Porter's imaginative lyrics, "Birds do it, bees do it, even educated fleas do it. . .," he was writing about falling in love. But here I am speaking of what birds and bees and educated fleas also do, which is to procreate.

Before, during, and after you have spoken to each other, you'll be making love in the hope of creating the love of your life, your baby. This act will be different than having sex, which is fine if your goal is, well, having sex. But once you have decided to create a life, the sex act takes on a spiritual magnitude. It is no longer a spirited venture with a satisfying orgasm in mind. That may be part of it, to be sure, but now, with the prospect of a new life twinkling in your eyes, it is even more.

It is more because this is simply the most creative and important thing that you'll ever do. Yes, getting college degrees or pursuing a satisfying career or engaging in philanthropy or serving your country or creating a work of art—all are spectacular things to do in a life. In fact, these creative, consequential, life-affirming acts are what fuel society.

But none compare to creating a baby. This is not a theory. It is the ancient and acknowledged wisdom of the ages. Even the piercing scientific inquiry into our genome—the entire map of our genetic inheritance— cannot be compared to the creation of a life, a miracle that continues to stand as an enigma of unfathomable depths. This is why making love to create a baby deserves the most special place in your busy lives.

"But how can we make love in a way that is more special than it has ever been before?" you may ask. In the same way that you have prepared yourselves in other ways. If you have already made sure that you are physically and emotionally healthy (a must), and you have made sure to establish that spiritual space, the next step is preparing your love bed—the bed in which your priceless baby will be conceived.

Creating Your Love Bed

For Comfort, Love, Sex, and Conception

To be sure, zillions of babies have been conceived to the absolute astonishment of their parents. How many times have we heard a mother-to-be exclaim, "I took my pills faithfully" or "I never even kissed my husband unless I had my diaphragm in" or "I thought it was the safe time of the month"? Some, perhaps many, of these babies were not conceived in a bed of love nor even in a bed, for that matter.

Having been a childbirth instructor for nearly two decades and before that an obstetrical nurse, I can say with some authority that for a positive outcome of pregnancy (that is, a healthy baby), conception does not have to take place under ideal conditions. Even casual observation, or the reading of practically anyone's biography, makes it clear that not everyone is conceived in idyllic circumstances, that there are vast populations of people living productive, contributory, happy lives whose beginnings were less than ideal.

While it certainly would be ideal if both parents were physically, mentally, and spiritually healthy before their baby is conceived, it is also true that the events that follow conception—pregnancy, childbirth, and parenting—are extremely important determinants of a healthy (and happy) baby.

Nevertheless, the more positive all the aspects of your life are as you embark on the quest to conceive, the better. Certainly, love must be counted among the most vital ingredients in creating a new life. This may seem so obvious as to be unnecessary to mention. Even when a couple loves each other very much, however, lovemaking is not always the relaxed, pleasurable, creative, or loving experience that God intended it to be—especially when engaged in by a busy, preoccupied, modern couple.

Challenges to a Loving Relationship

Maintaining a loving relationship—and a loving love life—is a great challenge for couples who work hard all day and endure the pressures of the workplace. Their energies may be depleted or their self-esteems battered, and when they return home each evening to face domestic chores and family responsibilities, it may seem impossible to find the time to be loving or to make love. Often, in fact, the only place where they can let their hair down and be real is in the privacy of their homes, where pent-up emotions may come tumbling out, only to land squarely on the last person who deserves them—their partners.

Of other challenges that assail the modern couple, finances are high on the list. It is no secret that the prime source of dissension among couples is money; hence, its sometimes-undeserved reputation as the root of all evil. Even if couples have worked out a division of labor and a way to share their earned incomes, money issues have a way of negating former agreements and tainting what otherwise would be a great relationship. Cherie and Chuck are an example.

Cherie came from a hardworking family that struggled to make ends meet. One of six children, she had worked since her teenage years and prided herself on having paid her own way through college and grad school to earn a master's degree in communications. When she met Chuck, she was an assistant producer at a local TV station. Her impressive job title, however, was not reflected in her paycheck. But, accustomed to stretching a dollar, Cherie still managed to establish a savings account and find bargains for her home and wardrobe.

Chuck's background was unlike Cherie's in every way. One of two children, his father was a surgeon and his mother a partner in a prominent law firm. Chuck often amused his friends by saying, "I'm the only person I know who grew up never hearing about money." Chuck worked in a financial firm and, at the age of 31, was making well over $100,000 a year.

You might guess that Cherie would have been thrilled not to have to worry about money, but she wasn't. At least three or four nights a week, Chuck would call to tell her that they were going out to dinner, either with clients or alone. In spite of her best intentions, Cherie would find herself sulking through dinner, and their evenings always ended in an argument. "I could have cooked that dinner for a quarter of the price," she would say to Chuck. "Why do we have to waste all that money?" Chuck would become furious and accuse Cherie of ruining the pleasures that a good income afforded them. They would both go to bed feeling bad.

Cherie and Chuck finally sought marriage counseling but quit before they had worked this problem out. One evening, while they were entertaining an important client of Chuck's in a fancy restaurant, Cherie spotted a spider scurrying along the floor and moved to squash it. But the client's wife, Cassie, stopped her—to everyone's horror. "Spiders are really quite fantastic," Cassie said.

An avid gardener, Cassie went on to tell her now-rapt audience of the wonders of a half-dozen other maligned and misunderstood creatures. "The thing is," she explained, "every creature is what it's supposed to be, to do what it's supposed to do. That's the way God designed the universe. So when we see something we're afraid of, or something we don't like, it's not because it's bad, it's because we don't understand it."

On the drive home, Chuck turned affectionately to Cherie. "Maybe you're just a little spider, and I'm just a little...cockroach." They both laughed because they both got it. By accepting Cassie's remarks in the way they were intended, they had gone a long way in accepting each other. It wasn't long before Cherie realized that she had been dragging her anxieties about money from the past into a present in which they were no longer relevant. Chuck, too, began to appreciate Cherie's talent for saving money (something he had neglected to do). They had opened themselves up to the lessons of God and nature and, in the process, had enriched their lives.

But this is just one story—with a happy ending. Money problems have many variations, as do problems of jealousy, of disparate interests in recreational activities, of sharing domestic responsibilities. . .the list goes on. Almost invariably, problems that exist before a child is born persist or get worse. So, while you are checking out your health, it is a good idea to address any problem in your relationship that may be a source of irritation, anger, or depression, and to remember that God is unerring.

The interest rate on the investment that you make in your relationship can be 100 percent and yield you returns that will last your whole life. One enduring truth about problems is that, in almost every case, they have solutions. And if they can't be completely fixed, most of them can be improved.

How wonderful to conceive a baby when you and your partner are in sync about the important issues that affect your life together. And what a perfect time to create the love bed in which your amazing baby will be conceived.

A Bed of Love

Although the love bed that you create may be the same bed in which you take a nap, watch television, or recover from a flu, it takes on special significance when you make love, especially if your goal is to conceive a baby. Now it becomes a *spiritual* love bed, because you and your partner are bringing to it your awareness of just how special this exhilarating and sacred venture is. This is how to make that special bed.

Create a Special Environment

Every single time you decide to go to bed to "make a baby," try to remember that this is the most important time that you have ever spent together. Before making love, spend some moments to enhance all of your physical, emotional, and spiritual faculties. Take a warm bath together. Massage each other with aromatic oils. Play music that is inspiring and romantic. All the while, try your best to think good thoughts, to visualize things that you consider life-affirming: a budding rose, a cuddly puppy, that child you saw in the park, a sunset. These thoughts and sexual fantasies are certainly not mutually exclusive—have both.

Anna and Rob tried these strategies, not initially to conceive, but to improve their sex life. Although they wanted a baby, the time that they spent in bed had become so unsatisfying that it was beginning to affect their whole relationship. They both knew enough to try to solve this problem before having a baby.

"I did everything," Anna said, "from reading books to buying sexy nightgowns to trying every fantasy imaginable, but nothing worked. When Rob and I were dating, I was a warm, sexy woman, but as soon as I got married, I turned into my mother, who was cold and never failed to tell me that 'marriage was legalized prostitution.' As soon as I said, 'I do,' I turned into an ice statue, just like her."

Anna and Rob tried couples therapy with a behavioral therapist, but in spite of their best efforts, Anna remained frozen. The love she and Rob felt for each other began to deteriorate. One weekend, they joined their friends Lisa and Jon on a camping trip to upstate New York. Over dinner and wine one evening, Anna and Rob told them of their sexual difficulties. Lisa, an environmental conservationist known by her friends to be somewhat of a philosopher, responded immediately. "I can help you," she said.

The next day, she led Anna and Rob to a spot in the forest and pointed to a huge tree. "Just sit here and look at that tree," she said. "It will tell you all the answers." Then she left them alone. Anna and Rob thought this very strange, but, having nowhere else to go, lent themselves to the exercise. After 2 hours, Lisa returned and asked them, "What do you see?"

"It's a very big tree," Rob said. "It has outstretched branches and wonderful leaves," Anna remarked. "What else?" Lisa asked. When Anna and Rob could think of nothing else, Lisa advised them to continue to look at the tree. When she returned a couple of hours later, she again asked them what they saw. "The tree is bent in the middle. It goes straight up and then curves sharply and then continues to the sky," Anna said.

Lisa nodded. "Why do you think that is?" she asked. Anna and Rob were at a complete loss. "I'll tell you," Lisa said. "It's because trees depend on sunlight for nourishment and growth. If they don't get enough sun, they naturally gravitate to where the sun is shining. Do you see the bend in this tree? It changed its shape to find the sun and to grow toward the sky. That's the way humans grow, too." All at once, Anna leaped to her feet. "That's me," she exclaimed. "I'm just like that tree."

"You've solved your problem," Lisa said to Anna and Rob. And they had. By tapping into the great wisdom of the universe, by opening themselves up to nature's lessons, they had found the answer to their problem in the crooked tree.

Indeed, Anna, like the tree, had been deprived of a great source of nourishment but had used her life-affirming drive to change direction and find the ability to love and be loved. Without completely understanding how the image of the tree had affected her, she found herself increasingly responsive sexually and, to both her own and Rob's delight, conceived a baby just three months later.

Anna's story demonstrates an important point about the nature of spiritual revelation. It does not require intellectual insight to see the light. Often, insights are absorbed into one's very being and translated into marvelous changes.

Take a Moment

Before you make love, take a few moments to acknowledge that your lovemaking is intended to create a life. Remember that the love you have for each other will be directly translated into the script that you're writing for your baby's new life. Say a prayer.

Thank you, God, for giving me life and health, for giving my partner life and health, and for blessing us with the life and health of our child-to-be.

Enjoy Every Minute

When you actually make love, try to enjoy every minute. If, for one of any number of reasons, your lovemaking is not as enjoyable as you had hoped, keep in mind that making love is not a contest in which the only important result is an orgasm or conception.

If loving and caring are present, these will prevail. Too often, couples who don't conceive right away interpret the lack of conception as a reflection of some inadequacy on their part. Their lovemaking becomes riddled with tension, and their efforts to conceive become mechanical. Of course, if many months go by and conception hasn't taken place, it's a good idea to consult a fertility expert for an evaluation.

Appreciate the Here and Now

Conception is a gift from God. When you are striving to be the recipient of this gift, it is a wonderful time to acknowledge the many gifts that you already possess. Recognize the bounty that surrounds you, including the fact that you are young enough and healthy enough to be engaged in this effort.

Make Your Love Bed Aesthetically Inviting

Just as the emotional and spiritual aspects of a love bed are important, so are its aesthetic qualities. People are largely ruled by their senses. Yes, character counts, as does intellect and other God-given qualities. But it is sight, hearing, touch, smell, and taste that are closest to our sexual, passionate natures, that are the prime catalysts in the affairs of our hearts.

How much more appetizing is a plate that offers food that not only is nutritious but also has a tantalizing flavor, an enticing aroma, and some dashes of color? How much more alluring is the man or woman whose hair shines, whose breath is sweet, and whose body exudes the scent of natural sexiness or even perfume? And how much more welcoming is a home in which chairs are comfortable, lighting is warm, and people are cordial and friendly? All these stimulate our senses and make us receptive to our surroundings.

It is the same with a love bed. Does your bedroom exude an inviting warmth? Is the lighting adaptable, not only for reading and discriminating between blue shoes and black, but for creating a romantic mood? Are your sheets and pillowcases clean and attractive? Has your bed been straightened so you can turn down the covers each night and snuggle into this cozy retreat to make love and to sleep?

Can you turn off the ring switch on your phone or put your phone in a drawer, the better to leave your day behind you? If you already have children, do you have a lock on your door to ensure that your privacy is not invaded? As any parent knows, a lack of privacy guarantees that a wonderful sexual experience will not take place.

In essence, is your bedroom a sanctuary that you associate with relaxation, with love, with sex, with the prospect of conceiving a child? If not, then make it a top priority to create this kind of haven. Better to leave dishes in the sink, recycling receptacles full, laundry unfolded, and calls unreturned. They will get done.

The love bed that you create and the atmosphere that you establish will provide you with a true respite from the rest of the world. Best of all, it will help to give you the chance to express the deep love that you have for each other—emotionally, sexually, and spiritually. Here are some suggestions for making your love bed and your bedroom cozy, warm, and sexy.

Make It a Place for Both of You

Buy a special quilt or coverlet that both of you love. Even if your tastes are different, a meeting of the minds on this issue will ensure that the very sight of your bed will put both of you in a good mood—and in a mood for love.

> *Decorating their home was the only bone of contention between Louise and Lance. She, a New Englander by birth, had grown up in an old colonial home, with beamed ceilings, a Dutch door, a fireplace in the kitchen, a hitching post out in front, and two barns in the back. "I loved gingham and chintz, soft lighting, and Early American furniture," Louise told me, "but Lance was Mr. Less Is More."*
>
> *A native Chicagoan, Lance had grown up in a high-rise apartment. His father, he said, had his chair, and his mother, a minimalist artist, decorated their home, well, minimally. "I like a sleek, modern look, lots of space, lots of light," Lance said.*
>
> *Despite their differences, Louise and Lance managed to agree about the decor of their living and dining rooms, both compromising to make the other happy. But their bedroom was another story. She preferred ruffled curtains and a thick, downy quilt; he preferred blinds and a thermal blanket. "I wanted a bedroom with*

warmth and sexiness," Louise said, "but Lance kept saying that when the lights were out, it didn't make a difference."

Louise accepted Lance's attitude as a guy thing until they began to discuss having a baby. "I wanted our baby to be conceived in a beautiful environment," she explained, "and all of a sudden, our bedroom became a major issue." Reluctantly, Lance agreed to shop with Louise for something she promised him they would both like. She was delighted when he agreed with her choice of colors: soft gray, a touch of rose, and dashes of green. She didn't love the fact that he chose a blanket instead of a quilt, but she happily went along because the blanket had all the right colors. Lance refused to look at curtains but agreed to a swag that would frame the blinds. He also agreed to a color change for the blinds—from stark white to soft gray—as well as to Louise's choice of six cushy pillows for the bed.

"It wasn't my fantasy bedroom," Louise said, "but it was so much warmer and sexier than it had been." She bought an attractive lamp, hung some pictures that they both loved on the wall, and perfumed the room with potpourri. Years later, she partially credited the amazing quality of their two children to the warm and sexy bedroom in which they had been conceived.

Sights and Scents, Sensuality and Sex

Nothing in life is more ruled by the senses than sex. The very sight of the one you love, the very smell of his hair, the sound of that voice, the touch of that skin—all determine who meets, who mates, who procreates. No wonder romance itself is such a sensory and sensual experience, one that is certainly worthy of your best efforts when thoughts of a baby are twinkling in your eyes.

What a wonderful time to sprinkle your bedroom with

surprise gifts, a plate of sinful cookies, a bowl of ripe fruit, satiny bedclothes, and sentimental love notes—all visual delights, some of which also taste and feel good and warm the heart.

The aroma of lilac-scented potpourri brought Louise happy memories of her years in Vermont. Like most people, she found certain fragrances evocative, even arousing. Scents have both powerful and subtle effects, as anyone knows who has detected the smell of a robust spaghetti sauce or the breeze of seductive perfume. If you have a favorite scent—be it a bowl of dried flowers, a candle with the smell of peaches or vanilla, or a spray of perfume—make it part of your bedroom decor.

Aromatic massage oils are wonderful as well, to the nose and to the touch. Clean, air-dried sheets have their own sexy smell. And, of course, fresh flowers are universally irresistible. Treat yourself and your partner to these sensory, sensual, sexy stimuli. They will enhance your relationship, make your love bed rich with romance, and create the fertile environment in which you follow the biblical edict to "be fruitful and multiply."

Chapter Six

When It's Difficult to Conceive
Keeping Heart and Hope

I t's more difficult to make a love bed when you have tried and tried to conceive to no avail. But before any woman accepts that she is infertile, it is of crucial importance that both she and her partner be checked out at the same time. Just as women experience infertility, so do men.

Too often, a woman will subject herself to extensive diagnostic tests, even surgical procedures, only to find out—months or even years later—that her partner has the fertility problem. Save yourselves unnecessary grief by getting evaluated for potential problems at the same time. And remember, most infertility problems have solutions.

A Historical—And Modern—Problem

Infertility problems are at an all-time high because many women, particularly in industrialized countries, are starting their families after the age of 30, when they have a diminishing number of ripe, fertile eggs.

In times past, women who had difficulty conceiving suffered because of society's opinion of them as inadequate or deficient. Now that we have a greater understanding of the biological nature of infertility as it affects both women and men, popular opinion has changed, as have medical treatments that are able to help infertile couples become parents.

Even when conceiving is not difficult, many women find themselves in a high-risk category, either because they have a preexisting medical problem (such as diabetes, a seizure disorder, a cardiac problem, and so forth), or they have had multiple miscarriages. If pregnancy does occur in these cases, a woman must be under the care of a high-risk pregnancy specialist.

Most women don't know if an infertility problem exists until they try to get pregnant and, instead, get their periods. Sometimes the attempt to conceive goes on for months and months, sometimes for years and years. The tests that women undergo and the fertility drugs that they hope will result in conception often take all the joy out of their relationships. Lovemaking turns into having sex, a woman's partner comes to feel like a service station, and the relationship goes downhill.

Sometimes the failure to conceive is a result of the physiological changes brought about by anxiety, although modern medicine has not yet devised a way to visualize or chart this phenomenon. Like other reported maladies that later prove to hold true, there is no doubt that empirical research will help legitimize the reports that psychological stress leads to infertility.

The Mind–Body Connection

I had a glimpse of this mind-body connection when I worked nights as a delivery-room nurse. I remember many a doctor calling in the middle of the night to say, "My patient is having contractions every 4 minutes," which meant that she was in active labor.

Yet, more often than not, when the woman arrived, her contractions had stopped. "I've been having contractions for hours," she would cry in desperation, "but now they've disappeared." The nurses knew the contractions would resume, but we always wondered why they had stopped.

Years later, I learned that emotions play a big part in the process. When a woman who has progressed far enough in labor to be ready to go to the hospital actually hears her doctor say, "Okay, it's time," the reality of labor hits her. This is the big moment, the final step in her nine-month voyage, the leg of the journey that in her wildest dreams she thought would never arrive. Excited, nervous, overwhelmed, and terrified, she does what other people do involuntarily when they are faced with extraordinary circumstances. She manufactures geysers of stress hormones, including epinephrine and norepinephrine. Interestingly enough, these hormones have an inhibiting effect on oxytocin and other chemicals that fuel the contractions of labor. So, of course, the contractions stop. But with Mother Nature progressing in her unstoppable way, they once again begin.

We can only speculate about how this relates to conception. We still don't know exactly how stress hormones affect conception, although there are untold numbers of stories about women who tried for years to conceive and, upon adopting a baby ("Whew, now I can relax") got pregnant.

Could it be that researchers have been looking for solutions to infertility in all the wrong places? Could incorporating a spiritual dimension into one's relationship and one's love bed be the answer? It's certainly worth exploring. And who better to conduct this exploration than the struggling couple?

Sometimes, couples decide to adopt a baby. But this once-common choice has become more difficult since the acceptability of single motherhood, the increased use of contraceptives, and legal abortion have lowered the availability of infants. The adoption process may take years and may even involve red-tape-filled trips to foreign countries. Complicated and time-consuming as adoption is, this, too, can wreak havoc on a relationship. Although if it ends happily, all the grief is soon forgotten.

Other couples pursue costly in vitro fertilization, in which the woman receives hormone treatments to increase her fertility, then enters a hospital (or fertility clinic) where her eggs (ova) are removed through a surgical laparoscopic procedure. After the eggs are fertilized by the sperm of her mate or a donor, they are implanted in her uterus, and the couple begins the anxiety-producing vigil to see if a pregnancy "takes." Again, this lengthy process often exacts a toll on the couple's relationship.

Still other couples opt for artificial insemination, in which a partner's or donor's sperm is collected, inserted through the cervix, and placed in the woman's uterus during her ovulatory cycle. Yet again, the wait to see if this technique works is nerve-wracking. In fact, during all of these efforts, it is not uncommon for both partners to feel like laboratory specimens themselves.

These are hardly the kind of circumstances that encourage the making of a love bed. But does that have to be the case? Absolutely not. The creation of a baby is life's most important act, one that deserves the participation of two loving people. Whether or not the egg and sperm from that couple are implanted in a bed or in a laboratory makes not one whit of difference. These are still the magical ingredients that will result in the birth of their precious baby.

If you are undergoing fertility treatments, by all means make your love bed with enthusiasm and optimism. Here's how to do it.

Remember Love

A love bed is a bed in which love is alive. If you've arrived at the point of accepting treatment for infertility, then "leave unto Caesar what is Caesar's." Trust that you have made the wisest choice and don't enter every love-making encounter with a maybe-this-time mentality. The surest path to inhibition, this is the way to turn a potentially passionate encounter into feelings of inadequacy or self-doubt. The love that you feel for one another will be translated into every cell of your body and, by association, into the heart and soul of your child-to-be, however that child is conceived.

Don't Get Upset

In going for in vitro fertilization or artificial insemination, you may feel aggravated every time you have trouble finding a parking space or anxious when you think about the time it's taking away from other pressing commitments or defensive about your adequacy. These are perfect times to call upon your spiritual awareness, to turn each of these trips into an opportunity to see things in a new way.

"Sure," you may say, "easier said than done." And you're right. Lofty philosophies are usually espoused by people who have triumphed over their troubles, not by those who are going through them. But consider Catherine, a woman who struggled with infertility for years.

Glistening Eyes

Catherine told me about her awakening spiritual awareness and how it had made a difference when she went through the in vitro process on two different occasions (both of which resulted in conception). She described how impossible it was for her to feel anything but irritation when she initially started her treatments. A paralegal in a Manhattan law firm, she spent her days preparing legal briefs, dashing from meeting to meeting, and taking buses, subways, and cabs from her office to the courts. "I wanted a baby more than anything," she said, "but when it was time for my in vitro appointments, all I could think about was the work that was piling up and the overtime hours I'd have to spend catching up."

One day, she said, she was waiting for a subway train when she saw a distraught little boy crying inconsolably. A transit policeman was helping him look for his mother, and Catherine volunteered to help the search. The policeman asked the four-year-old what color his mother's coat was or if she was carrying a pocketbook. Gasping between sobs, he answered as best he could.

Then Catherine stooped down and asked the frantic little boy what his mommy looked like. All of a sudden, he stopped crying and Catherine could see him searching his memory to summon up a mental image of his mother. Then, she recalled, his eyes began to glisten and a hint of a smile appeared upon his face. "Pretty," he answered, "my mommy pretty."

"I was spending my life around people whose eyes never glistened," Catherine told me, "and here, right in front of me, was what life was all about." This image affected her profoundly. After that, she remembered the little boy's face whenever she went to her in vitro

appointments. "I used to think about his sparkling eyes,"
she said. "His face became the image of the child I hoped
to have."

Keep Heart!

Waiting for the results of fertility treatments can be un-bearably anxiety-producing. As a woman watches her cal-endar for the date that her period is due, she starts to hesitate every time she goes into the bathroom, dreading to see the first drops of blood that signal the start of another period. However successful these treatments have been for thousands of women, some of them still don't take.

If you are disappointed, keep heart. Thinking twice to reinterpret an experience will help you place it in perspec-tive and approach it again, perhaps, with renewed vigor. At this stage of what is known—and not known—about the mysterious process of conception, the failure of fertility treatment is not entirely understood. It may be the result of one small missing link in your own state—spirituality perhaps?—or of the limitations of the methods so far de-veloped, methods that cannot yet ensure the desired result.

Of course, knowing where the limitations lie does not diminish the pain. But, spiritually thinking, there is an-other way to interpret your disappointment, to trust that what science, medicine, and technology don't yet under-stand, God does.

Making Lemons into Lemonade

Fleury illustrates this thinking perfectly. The co-owner of a paper-goods manufacturing plant, Fleury told me that she had always believed a sign that she had hung in her office embodied her philosophy of life, but that until she went through artificial insemination, she had never really reflected on its true meaning.

"Every day," she said, "I took for granted a sign on the wall in front of me—'When Life Gives You Lemons, Make Lemonade.' I'd only think of it to rationalize the fact that when a bad cold kept me out of work, I had the chance to clean some closets."

When Fleury was artificially inseminated and didn't get pregnant, she became deeply depressed. "It seemed like the worst thing that ever happened to me," she said, "even worse than the all the years that my husband and I had tried to have a baby, even worse than the tests I went through. This was it. And when it failed, I thought I'd never smile again."

Dragging herself to work each day, Fleury found herself staring blankly into space, hating every invoice that passed her desk, recoiling at every fax transmission, avoiding every phone call. One day, she realized that she had been gazing mindlessly at the poster.

"There it was, right in front of me for all these years, and I had never really seen it," she exclaimed in amazement. "All at once, I realized that my disappointment was the lemons, but that I was dying of thirst because I hadn't been wise enough to make myself even one drop of lemonade." At that moment, Fleury decided to make a list, recounting all of the things that she had learned and the ways that she had changed from her disappointing experience. Number one was empathy, followed by patience and strength.

"I realized that I had become a better person through my own pain," she said with genuine pride. "This may have started when I couldn't get pregnant, but when the artificial insemination didn't take, I started to feel more compassion for other people's problems. Then I realized that I had been very strong in going through all those months of tests, and for the first time in my life, I began to think of myself as a real survivor in the war of life."

By viewing her experience from a spiritual perspective, Fleury had made her own lemonade. She still had, however, one quality to add to her list—resilience. Once Fleury's glass was spiritually full, she tried artificial insemination again and today is the mother of a cherished little girl.

Both Catherine and Fleury, in struggling with infertility problems, arrived at spiritual awareness through different routes. Significantly, it was the issue of motherhood that brought about the global changes they experienced. Why is this significant? Because insight, genuine insight, is catalyzed by the truly momentous questions that we ask ourselves about what is important in life—and by the evolved answers that everyone is capable of providing for themselves.

So when your eyes are twinkling with the promise of a baby, try diligently to include spiritual thinking in your everyday thoughts. See yourself as a priceless part of the universe that you inhabit. Take time to appreciate the grandeur and mystery of nature. And consider the love you have within you and the love you have for each other a gift that you will pass along to your child—be that child born of lovemaking, in vitro fertilization, artificial insemination, or adoption.

Chapter Seven ✳

The Miracle of Conception
Life's Awesome Beginning

Several years ago, I heard of an American woman named Gloria who received a phone call that shocked her to her very bones. Forty years before, while World War II raged overseas, Gloria had written to a pen pal in France, a young schoolgirl named Angelique. They exchanged stories about their families, their doll collections, and their very different experiences during the war years—Gloria, living an untroubled life in a safe land, and Angelique, cowering from the sounds of bombing raids and suffering through food shortages.

Although she continued to think about Angelique, their correspondence ended when Gloria's family moved from the Midwest to New York and she entered junior high school. When Angelique was about 12 and visiting relatives in the south of France, she wrote one last note to

Gloria, placed it inside a Coca-Cola bottle, and threw it with abandon into the Atlantic Ocean.

Forty years later, a beachcomber on the shores of Maine found the Coke bottle wedged between some jutting rocks. To his astonishment, the note inside the bottle was still legible, and he decided to track down the person to whom it was addressed—none other than Gloria.

After tracking down Gloria's elderly mother, he was finally able to contact Gloria. When Gloria recovered from the shock of receiving the note from her long-lost friend, she tried to track down Angelique. It took another two years, including a trip to France, but, remarkably, she succeeded. When the two finally met, each one called it the most amazing experience of their lives.

They hugged and kissed and cried and held long conversations about all the capricious events that had gone into their stranger-than-life reunion: the durability of the Coca-Cola bottle, the long-lasting nature of the ink, the whimsical tides that had directed the bottle to America, the perseverance of the beachcomber in tracking down Gloria, Gloria's own persistence in pursuing Angelique, and the pure good fortune that they were both still alive and healthy and able to see this story to its happy end.

Certainly, the chances of Angelique's note ever reaching Gloria were, by any measure, less than one in a million. And yet, this unlikely happening pales in comparison to an event that most of us take for granted and, in fact, consider quite ordinary. That event is conception, the beginning of human life.

Why do we gasp at a story like Gloria's but hardly blink an eye when hearing of a pregnancy? Wherever we look, we see hordes of people or hear about overpopulation or read about the baby boom sweeping our nation. No wonder we simply smile and say "Congratulations" when we learn that someone we know is pregnant. It's not exactly like finding a note in a Coke bottle after 40 years.

Conception's Window of Opportunity

Conception is far more astounding than finding a long-lost letter. Even before conception takes place, truly wondrous events are at work. First, there are the untold numbers of circumstances that must be in harmony before the work of art that you and your mate are creating comes into being: the time of the month, the internal chemistry of the mother-to-be, the ripeness of her egg, the motility of the sperm, and the grace of God.

When all these elements coalesce, then literally millions upon millions of sperm (actually, an estimated 300 million in each ejaculation) swim steadfastly toward their goal—the solitary egg (or sometimes two or three eggs) that has emerged from the ovary and begun its own journey toward the uterus.

Many sperm will straggle along the way and others will perish, giving up the contest to their more hardy competitors. Others will attempt to prevail, each one making its way through the labyrinthine maze of cervix, uterus, and fallopian tube. This process may take place many times a month or, if you make love more frequently, even many times a day. But only during a few hours of each month—as few as 12, as many as 48—will the possibility of conception exist.

These are the hours of ovulation, the midway point in your menstrual cycle when one of the thousands upon thousands of eggs that you were born with leaves one of your tiny, almond-shaped ovaries to wend its way toward your uterus. Preceding the release of this egg, a delicate hormonal dance occurs, involving the exquisite coordination of the brain's hypothalamus and pituitary glands as well as the hormones of the ovaries and uterus.

At this time, the hormones estrogen and progesterone, which are produced in the ovaries, course through your system until they reach the perfect crescendo. By the time ovulation takes place, their magical effects will have created a soft, thick, luxuriant uterine lining—rich in nutrients, hormones, and blood vessels—ready to receive the microscopic embryo that will develop into your baby.

But even before ovulation, powerful forces are taking place. About two days before your egg is released, while it is still contained in a protective envelope called a vesicle, meiosis begins. This incredible process of cell division matures the egg and its genetic material, the chromosomes that contain half of the characteristics that your child will inherit. The same process has taken place in the sperm. Once the egg is released, it is encircled by nutritive cells that feed and sustain it as its journey begins.

None of these events—or the thousands of other biochemical and physical processes that, in all women, have the potential to create life—are visible to the naked eye. Taking place outside our awareness, they are guided by a force so immense and incomprehensible that we can only wonder at its magnitude. This wonder, this affirmation that an all-knowing God is guiding these mysterious processes, is the spiritual dimension that endows conception with the awe and humility it warrants.

How does it all work, the magnificent creation of a human life? How, possibly, with all the variables it involves, does anyone get pregnant? It almost begs the imagination to realize that even when you are just thinking about having a baby, these amazing processes are at work—every day, every week, every month, for more than 30 years of a woman's life.

What a wonderful time to direct your attention to the ways in which your own amazing body relates, cell by cell, to the precious, fragile, equally amazing body of your baby; to contemplate the mystery of conception; to envision the invisible process of cell division; and to pray that it takes place as God and nature designed it.

The Magical Moment of Beginning Life

As your egg is in transit, about 100 amorous sperm that have weathered their competition now approach it and avidly begin to pare away the egg's outer layer of cells. For hours and hours, their tails flagellating wildly, the sperm try to penetrate the ovum's outer wall. And then—poof— *one* succeeds.

In one imperceptible moment, through a process that sophisticated scientists are only now on the brink of understanding, that one sperm and that one most-desired egg come together. All sorts of complex enzymatic and chemical reactions are at work here, signaling the beginning of your child's life. And so covetous of this moment is that one egg that it instantly turns off access to other still-hopeful sperm.

After a journey of less than a day, and abetted by an almost incredible confluence of circumstances, the mother's and father's chromosomes blend together, establishing their baby's entire genetic inheritance. At this awesome moment, both chromosomes and genes are inextricably united to endow your baby-to-be with all the qualities that he or she will carry through life. Like birds on a wire, more than 100,000 genes reside on the 46 chromosomes of our genetic inheritance, carrying with them the intricate design, the blueprint, of the people we are and the people we will ultimately produce.

In that one fraction of a millisecond, the history of the world has changed. Now, even though you will not be aware that conception has taken place for several weeks or more, the universe is a different place—a place in which the unique child who will make his or her appearance in several months has begun to develop, to grow, to become.

At the moment of conception, your child's gender is determined. Although maleness or femaleness do not become visibly evident for several weeks into embryological development, and you may not learn if your baby is a boy or a girl until birth (or until a sonogram or amniocentesis reveals this confidence), this secret of nature, this wonderment of wonderments, is already known to God.

The complex, mysterious biological phenomenon of conception is humbling enough. When one thinks that here we are at the brink of a new century, evolved beyond our wildest imaginations, exploring the farthest reaches of space and the deepest chasms of the oceans, but just beginning to learn about the very stuff of which life is made, we know that the spirit of God is alive and well in the universe.

It is certainly no mystery why synonyms for the word *conceive* include *invent, originate,* and *imagine.* Indeed, the magnificent individual that you and your mate are creating is, in the history of the world, like no other. But we speak here only of the moment of conception and not of the cascade of miracles that takes place after this world-changing event.

In the days following the moment of conception, the now-united sperm and egg continue to develop rapidly. Two cells become 4, 4 become 8, and this tiny mass of cells is propelled down the winding corridor of your fallopian tube by the unstoppable action of tiny, hairlike projections called cilia. Cell division goes on and on to 16 cells, 32 cells, 64 cells and finally, on the seventh day—significantly, the time it took for God to create the universe—implantation takes place.

All of this vibrant life has been taking place within you, yet you don't yet know you're pregnant. But wouldn't this be an excellent time to think about what might be happening inside you, to pray to God that if you have conceived, nature is taking its normal course and the teeny, tiny cells of your little one are dividing as they should and progressing with the kind of smooth passage that you hope he will have through life?

After all, even before you learn that you're pregnant, your newly conceived child has been hard at work, striving to establish a relationship with you that will last for a lifetime. That work does not stop with implantation. Now that this priceless fertilized egg has reached your uterus, even more work begins. First, this tiny creature, still considered pre-embryonic, must establish a bloodline in the cushiony bed on which it has landed within your uterus.

Just like fully developed adults who put down roots in a community, your pre-embryonic child has been reaching out, implanting the slender vessels of the chorionic villi into your bloodstream. At this time, the cells of the villi begin to produce even more progesterone, the hormone that, according to the meaning of its name (*pro-*, "for," and *-gesterone*, "gestation"), will promote and sustain your pregnancy.

From this blood connection will flow everything that sustains life: the nutrients that your little one takes into its system, the exchange of gases that will preserve its life, the hormones that will fuel its development, and the deep emotional bond that will flow to and from mother to child throughout both of their lives.

Praise and Humility

All these remarkable processes are taking place, yet you still don't know that you're pregnant. Again, this seems a perfect time to reflect on these astounding phenomena and to tap into your spiritual awareness, imagining what is happening within you and acknowledging the miracle of it all.

"Well," you may say, "it's kind of hard to thank God for an invisible process that may or may not be taking place." That is true. On the other hand, we're all accustomed to saying thank you for things that are significantly less worthy of our gratitude. How many of us—without so much as a thank-you in return—express gratitude to a shopkeeper for a bag of groceries or to a receptionist for making an appointment or to a doctor for telling us to lose weight? And how many of us thank God for a raise, an ego-boosting honor, or even a two-dollar lottery win?

Certainly, then, just the possibility that this wonderful event may be in the works is reason enough to offer praise to the transcendent power that guides the whole process. This may take the form of reflective thought or simple prayer. In acknowledging the miraculous process of conception and in endowing it with reverence and respect, you will enter a realm of spiritual pregnancy that will infuse your entire experience with meaning and joy.

Even before you know that you're pregnant, you may find yourself looking with newfound curiosity at other pregnant women, marveling at the incredible happenstance that brought about their pregnancies. When you contemplate this and relate it to your own hoped-for pregnancy, you may find yourself starting to experience the first stirrings of maternal protectiveness, the desire to do everything possible to safeguard your child from harm. What a wonderful way to enter parenthood—to consider the very embryonic beginning of your child's life for the very humbling, God-given miracle that it is.

Chapter Eight

Learning the Good News
"Am I Pregnant?"

ome women know they're pregnant even before they have missed a period. They are so attuned to the delicate rhythms of their bodies that they can sense the oh-so-subtle changes that signal the new life within them. Yet others are not so regular, so the days that pass without a period leave them in a state of limbo—excited at each passing day but reluctant about getting too excited in case they're disappointed.

"I Thanked God, but I Got My Period"

You may be among the more than 40 percent of women who, in spite of their efforts, do not conceive on the first, second, or third try. Knowing how complex the whole process is, you surely understand that more than a million variables have to be in sync for pregnancy to take place. If you do not have a diagnosed infertility problem, trust that in just a few more efforts your egg and your partner's sperm will happily get together.

It is perfectly normal and understandable for anyone trying to get pregnant to feel devastated when weeks go by and, instead of missing a period, it arrives. Except for the rarest of circumstances, which now allow some post-menopausal women to become pregnant by implanting fertilized eggs into their uteruses and then sustaining their pregnancies with hormones, most women cannot become pregnant unless they get periods.

So, if you are menstruating, you are a candidate for pregnancy. If you are trying to get pregnant, embrace the spiritual thinking that acknowledges the amazing biological and emotional mechanisms that allow pregnancy to happen in the first place. And if you get your period, thank God as well. You and every one of your body's functions are part of the grand scheme of nature. Trust that whatever God sends your way has a purpose, a meaning, an intention. And enjoy your health and vitality and trying to the hilt. This is what life is all about.

"I Think I Missed My Period!"

Think? When a woman who wants to get pregnant says that she thinks she missed her period, that usually means she hopes she missed it. If you have gone past your normal 28-day cycle, then thinking you missed your period is probably true. In fact, you are probably pregnant. If your cycle is irregular, then it takes a little longer to find out. But, when any woman goes past what is normal for her cycle, she knows that pregnancy is a possibility.

In times past, a woman went to her doctor to learn if she was pregnant. Her urine specimen was sent to a laboratory to be tested on the stereotype of fast-breeding animals—rabbits. Many a woman from that era yearned to hear the words that confirmed her pregnancy: "The rabbit died."

Today, a woman routinely goes to her pharmacy, buys a pregnancy-test kit, and learns in the privacy of her own home whether or not she is carrying a child. If the result is positive, which means she's pregnant, she will probably reread the kit's directions several times, just to make sure that it really reads "positive."

After performing such a test, a woman usually rushes to her doctor or midwife to gain affirmation of her status. For the most part, a woman will know she's pregnant within a month or two after her baby has been conceived.

"Oh My Goodness, I'm Pregnant!"

I know women who have had 8 or 10 or 12 children, all of whom vividly remembered the exact moment they learned they were pregnant every time. It's the moment when everything female and powerful about her is confirmed and exalted. Intrinsically a spiritual experience, this is an event that allows every woman to know that she holds within her the potential to alter the course of the universe.

In fact, this is not grandiose thinking. We all know of the profound influence that mothers have on their children, although sometimes that influence is exaggerated or only cited to cast blame if a child's development is problematic. So it is important to remember that fully one-half of a child's genetic inheritance derives from the chromosomes and genes and psychological influences of its father.

If you have missed thanking God before you learned your good news, before you have fully appreciated the hard work that your pre-embryo—and now that you're pregnant, your actual embryo—has done to bring you to this festive point, then now is the time to hold each other closely and give thanks for this blessing.

Learning Your Due Date

However you receive the good news, one of the first things that you'll want to determine is your due date—that auspicious day when your baby will make its debut into the world. Actually, the length of pregnancy may vary widely, from 240 to 300 days. From the time of conception, its duration is generally 10 lunar months, or 36 to 40 weeks.

A generally accurate way to calculate your due date is to take the first day of your last period, count back three months, and add seven days. So if the first day of your last period was on December 9, count back three months to September 9, add seven days, and your due date will be September 16. Although this date is not etched in concrete, it is still exciting to learn the general time when you'll be celebrating your baby's birthday.

Learning of this milestone event is yet another lovely time for a spiritual reverie. If, before this moment, you have entertained the possibility that you might be pregnant and have contemplated the various amazing processes taking place inside you as the tiny embryo that will become your baby begins to develop, you have already begun to think spiritually.

You have already marveled at the thought that the coming together of an invisible sperm and a microscopic egg can result a mere nine months later in the delivery of a full human being. And you have already acknowledged the presence of a God more creative and powerful and benevolent than any other force in the universe.

You have done this knowing that everything that you are is inextricably intertwined with your offspring, and that spirituality is or will be as nourishing to your baby as any food, any thought, any exercise, any philosophy will ever be.

A Time for Meditation and Prayer

Now, certainly, is a time to reflect on the arduous journey your child-to-be has taken, the stamina it has required for him or her to have arrived safely in the protective environment of your uterus. At this profound moment, you and your partner will need time to comprehend the enormity of the life-changing events that have taken place.

Sitting together in silence, allowing your thoughts and feelings to emerge, thinking about the vastness of the universe and the immensity of your baby's place in the universe, try to capture these deep and spiritual moments and retain them forever.

During your meditation, you may have the desire to thank God for smiling down upon you. Here is one prayer that you may choose.

Dear God, the creator of the universe and of life itself....
Thank you for helping our child with the hard work that he has done to arrive at this wonderful moment.
Thank you for helping us with the hard work that we have done to bring our precious child's life to this point of development.
Thank you for endowing us with healthy minds and bodies, which we will care for so that our developing child will receive the benefits of our efforts.
We ask you, God, to bless us with your wisdom and goodness for our child's safe passage through the complicated processes of pregnancy and birth.
And we ask you, God, to guide us in your wisdom and goodness as we raise our precious child throughout his life.

The fact that you are pregnant means that one of your prayers has already been answered. God will answer your prayers of supplication and gratitude. Never forget that.

Mixed Feelings

The good news of a pregnancy can inspire some mixed feelings as well. In fact, even when a couple has thrown away their birth control and consciously planned a baby, actually learning that they have conceived often evokes an avalanche of emotions. When the reality of their new status as parents-to-be sinks in, and they realize that their lives will be dramatically and irrevocably changed forever, it is not uncommon for ambivalent feelings to rise to the surface—emotions that may come as a surprise to the couple who anticipated feeling nothing but joy.

During one of my Lamaze classes, the subject of such ambivalence arose. A young mother-to-be, Deborah, told the class that she had always dreamed about having a baby, but that when she learned she was pregnant, she was shocked by her reaction. "All of a sudden, all I thought about were the negatives," she said. "Would I be losing my freedom? Would I feel trapped? Would it affect my marriage? Did I really want to stay home for two months? I really loved my job."

She was reassured by the assenting nods of the class members, but not as much as when Christof, a relatively older father-to-be, affirmed what she had said by citing an example that, initially, everyone thought was funny. "Oh, I learned all about that in college," he exclaimed. Everyone giggled at his remark because no one else in the class had learned about the mixed feelings they had about conception in college.

But Christof continued with this example. "When I

was at the end of my second year," he explained, "all of a sudden, I got a form that said, 'Fill out your choice of major.' My major! This meant that I had to decide what I wanted to do with the rest of my life." Saying that he had always been "an upbeat guy," Christof described his anxiety. "Here, I was going to college to prepare myself for life, but the first 'life decision' I had to make threw me for a loop."

He soon learned that most of his classmates were feeling the same. "In fact, they called it the sophomore slump," he said. "It wasn't only me, it was everyone. So it's the same thing with having a baby. You learn something good, and you know you should be feeling happy, but then the reality of the whole thing hits you—boom."

By the time Christof finished speaking, everyone in the class was nodding and laughing and citing examples of their own ambivalent feelings. But Christof had one more thing to add. "The thing I learned," he said, "is that all of the big things in life make you feel up and down—great one minute, scared the next, happy, sad, even angry. That's why they're called the big things in life. So now, anytime something big happens, I know to expect it."

Christof's testimony in its simply stated way was the essence of wisdom. He had been able to translate one traumatic circumstance into a profound lesson about life itself. And he had been able to apply that lesson to other, even more trying, events in his life. His wife, Ingrid, confirmed this. Sitting shyly beside her gregarious husband, she had said little. But when the class turned to her, she spoke up.

"I felt a lot like Deborah," Ingrid said. "The same mixed feelings, good and bad. But every time I cried to

Christof, he just put his arms around me and told me that whatever I was feeling was okay." In just a few words Ingrid had spoken of the power of love and the wisdom that derives from understanding and accepting the human condition. God made us, with all of our fearfulness and confidence, stubbornness and adaptability, strength and vulnerability.

It is no mystery that couples who learn that they're to become parents feel some ambivalence. Mixed emotions arise almost every day over issues significantly less consequential, from choosing the color of a blouse to making an appointment with a dentist. Even about deeper issues, however, it is the nature of our species to entertain several— often conflicting—feelings.

These mixed feelings are commonly recognized as only human, yet when it comes to the global event of becoming a parent, many mothers- and fathers-to-be (as well as society at large) believe that the only appropriate responses are joy and elation. When less sanguine feelings arise, they are bewildered and upset.

Well, no more. Whatever you feel, treat yourself and each other with understanding and benevolence. Try to accept and understand and gain insight into your feelings. After all, you have participated in one of the most momentous events in human existence. Over time, as your pregnancy progresses, the initial ambivalence that you feel will subside or disappear. Inevitably, other feelings will emerge, some of them ambivalent as well.

Throughout the next nine months, the strength of your relationship will help you weather both the physical and emotional challenges that pregnancy presents. The spiritual space you have established, your increasing appreciation of the miracle of life, and your continuing relationship with God—all these will guide you through the uncharted course that you are just beginning.

The First Blush of Pregnancy

The initial exhilaration—or ambivalence—upon learning that you are pregnant is only the preamble to the torrent of emotions that will follow. Unlike the excitement that accompanies most thrilling events, which inevitably fades with the passage of time, the first blush of pregnancy increases. From the moment you learn that you're pregnant, this knowledge remains preeminent in your mind and heart.

The most ordinary daily behavior—brushing your teeth, eating breakfast, choosing an outfit, driving a car, having a conversation, even sneezing—all are accompanied by the keen awareness that, for the first time in your entire life (or the second or third or fourth, depending on which pregnancy this is), you are spending every second of your day, every moment of your night, with another human being.

And this is no ordinary human being. This is your child. Already, even before you have one sign or symptom of pregnancy, this tiny person within you is taking on astounding characteristics, responding to you in ways that you can only imagine.

Over the next days and weeks and months, you will get to know your little one even better. By understanding the wonderful things taking place during your first trimester, your maternal instincts will begin to develop, and you will look forward to each new change with awe, with excitement, and with a spiritual awareness that, yes, this, as Christof said, is truly one of "the big things in life."

Chapter Nine ❧

Getting to Know the New You

Sex, Mother Love, and Faith

As soon as you learn that you are pregnant, every moment of your life will be spent in the presence of another human being. You will think about this all the time and perceive yourself in new and wonderful ways. But it is not until anywhere from four to six weeks after conception that you will experience the first symptoms of pregnancy.

Unlike the symptoms of other conditions, which serve to tell you what is wrong, the symptoms of pregnancy signal what is right. Many symptoms are not particularly bothersome, but even when unpleasant or difficult, they can accurately be interpreted as an affirmative sign that your body is sustaining a human life.

The Telling Signs of Pregnancy ❧

Just as no two people are alike, neither are any two pregnancies. Even your own pregnancies will differ from one another. For all women, however, the most probable sign of pregnancy is a missed period. But because women miss periods for many reasons (some physical, others psychological), pregnancy must still be confirmed by a test.

For many women, one of the first symptoms of pregnancy is fatigue, the kind of all-over feeling of tiredness that makes you feel as though you never really woke up in the morning. Although common, this is a symptom that women—especially modern, overworked women—so rarely associate with pregnancy that they may chalk up their fatigue to everything from stress at work to a hectic weekend to the onset of their periods.

Some women, even very early in their pregnancies, experience the desire to urinate frequently. Even though the uterus is only slightly enlarged at this point, its close proximity to the bladder gives rise to this sensation, which diminishes over time but returns in later pregnancy when the uterus again presses on the bladder.

About 50 percent of women experience nausea and vomiting—morning sickness—which can also occur during the day and evening. Although this unpleasant symptom, which is thought to result from the effect of fluctuating hormone levels on the gastrointestinal tract, usually abates by the end of the third month, many women cope with it successfully by taking vitamin B_6, eating dry crackers, sipping ginger ale, and eating small, frequent, high-protein meals throughout the day.

Women also experience tenderness in and enlargement of their breasts, the kind of feeling that they have before their periods, only more exaggerated. Breast changes will continue throughout pregnancy as your body prepares for lactation and breast-feeding. In addition, your cervix, which is the bottom part of your pear-shaped uterus, will slowly undergo changes in vascularity and softness in preparation for delivery.

There may also be alterations in your mood. Just as estrogen and other hormones influence a woman's mood before her period, they can affect her mood when pregnant. You may feel a little weepy, or short-tempered, or, well, moody. Or, your mood may be elevated. I've met many women who have told me that even before they knew they were pregnant, they felt almost euphoric. Such are the wonders of estrogen.

Oh, Dad, Poor Dad . . .

While you experience these first symptoms of pregnancy, your partner may feel somewhat displaced. Although he may crow to his friends at work of his impending fatherhood, he may feel quite different at home. Rather than returning at the end of the day to a cheery greeting or an interesting conversation, and rather than looking forward to sharing a hearty meal or a comfortable evening in front of the TV, he may now find himself with someone who is nauseated by even the mention of food or exhausted or weepy. Worse, he may feel completely helpless to do anything that might make her feel better.

Displaced, helpless—it isn't easy. Just as pregnancy is physically and emotionally challenging for women, it can be difficult and demanding for men. When once they enjoyed being the center of attention or, at least, costarring in the spotlight with their partners, they now must take a backseat. And just when they may feel their most helpless, they are expected to give their partners a lion's share of understanding and empathy.

> *Tony said that he could feel himself "turning" when his wife, Julie, became pregnant. "I was always a nice guy," he said, "the life of the party, but also the first one to help out. In fact, when anyone I knew was going through something tough, they always called on me. So when Julie got pregnant, I thought I'd be great." But when Julie began to have morning sickness and then*

*temporary bleeding forced her into bed for two weeks,
Tony said that he felt like never going home.*

*"There were always plenty of people there—Julie's
mother, her sister, her best friend—but they all seemed to
know what to do, and I didn't. Every time I asked Julie
what I could do for her, she said 'nothing' and I just felt
in the way, like I didn't belong in my own home."*

*Tony was so naturally gregarious that he told just
about everyone how he felt and was lucky to happen
upon someone who helped him understand why he had
"turned" and what he could do about it. The source of
this wisdom came from Joey, the counterman at the local
deli. "I was going on and on about how I was a stranger
in my own home, and Joey said that I had it all
wrong—I wasn't the stranger, my baby was. He asked
me how I could treat a 'little helpless kid' like that."*

*Joey told Tony that his baby had "just moved into this
new home" (he meant Julie's body) and was "trying to get
comfortable. Maybe he's having a tough time, like you
are—he's already like his Dad." And "now both of you are
giving her grief. The baby is making her throw up, and
you're probably making her feel like throwing up, too."*

*"But when I try to help," Tony complained, "there's
nothing for me to do." Again, Joey disagreed. Without
phrasing his advice in spiritual terms, he essentially
gave Tony a blueprint for viewing Julie's pregnancy
and his unborn child's life in a spiritual way. "Do,
shmoo," he said. "Sit down next to her and do
nothing—just be there. Buy her some magazines that
she likes. Make sure the room's not too bright; pull down
the shades. Buy her some flowers; women like roses. Get
a naming-the-baby book; you'll both have fun, and it
will take her mind off her troubles. Hold her hand. Rub
her shoulders. Play some music. Say a prayer. Now, get
outta here, ya' big lug."*

*Tony was intrigued by Joey's reference to Julie as
their baby's new "home." He had never thought of the*

*embryo developing inside her as a real person, and
it occurred to him that maybe Joey was right, maybe
this "person" and Tony's wife were both trying to "get
comfortable." When he returned home—carrying
roses—he once again felt a part of his own home.*

Unlike Tony, there are men who feel such empathy and
identification with their partners that they develop early
pregnancy symptoms themselves. This well-documented
phenomenon is called *couvade*, which in French means "to
brood" or "to hatch." When it occurs, men join their pregnant partners in feeling fatigue or in developing the symptoms of morning sickness, insomnia, or stress.

An effective way to deal with the symptoms of pregnancy is to "think twice" about them, to see them, as Joey
suggested, in a new way. While many couples talk to their
babies before birth, this lovely communication often begins in later pregnancy. But why not start right away?

When you're fatigued, you might thank your little one
for being wise enough to slow you down. When you have
to urinate several times a day, you might visualize the
growth taking place that is causing your uterus to enlarge
and thank God that your baby's development is progressing. Even when you experience nausea, you can remind yourself that its cause is the hormonal activity that is
fueling your very important pregnancy. Your symptoms are
God's way of keeping you aware of and concerned about
the precious cargo that you're carrying. By experiencing
them as the gifts they are, you will be endowing your pregnancy with a spiritual sensibility that will increase richly in
the coming months.

What about Sex?

Another change that you may notice is your interest in
lovemaking. This, too, can vary from increased interest to

transitory noninterest. Particularly if a woman is experiencing nausea in early pregnancy, her desire for sex may be diminished or even nonexistent. When the nausea goes away after about three months and she enters her second trimester, she may feel quite sexy and amorous. Then, when other discomforts occur, such as heartburn or, in later pregnancy, hemorrhoids or a feeling of awkwardness and heaviness, she may again find her sexual interest waning.

Now is the time to communicate with your partner. The more he learns about the normal changes that take place in pregnancy, the better he will understand that sexuality, too, can have its ups and downs and that this in no way signals a blueprint for the future.

> *Susannah became a mother when she was 17 and her husband, Eric, was 20. They had been "madly in love," she told me, "and making love nonstop" when she became pregnant and lost all interest in sex. Instead of things getting worse, however, she described the way that Eric's reaction had positively shaped, not only her pregnancy experience but also their whole marriage.*
>
> *"I remember crying and crying," she said, "because I knew how important sex was to both of us, and I was afraid Eric wouldn't understand. I felt like something was wrong with me and that we'd have a terrible marriage. In fact, I thought I wouldn't even have a marriage because I wouldn't have blamed him for not wanting to live in a marriage without sex."*
>
> *One night, when Eric turned to Susannah in the hope of making love, she told him again that she "just wasn't in the mood." She told him how terrible she felt, but that she "couldn't help it."*
>
> *"Hey," he said. "I love you, so don't worry. We're going to be married forever, so we'll have plenty of time for this. Things will get better."*

In just three sentences, Eric had said all the right things. And things did get better. When I first met Susannah, she and Eric had been married for 22 years and were the parents of four children. Laughing, Susannah whispered to me, "And we're still making love nonstop."

As it happened, Eric had grown up on a farm in Minnesota. When I asked him how he had been so wise—at so young an age—to have known what to say to Susannah during her first pregnancy, he replied: "One thing you learn on a farm is that if you want healthy apples, you must have healthy trees—and you can't have healthy trees unless you respect nature. You also learn that when it comes to being born and being sick and dying, people and animals are very much the same. You have to give them time. I knew that Susannah needed time, and I knew we had time."

Eric went on to say that he had attended the birth of dozens of calves. He described the ways in which mother cows got to know and protect their offspring even before they were born. "They get restless and then they get quiet," he said, "as if they're aware that they're doing something very important." Eric was naturally attuned to the spiritual aspect of pregnancy and parenting. Having been instructed by nature itself, he was able to apply the lessons he had learned to his life—to the great benefit of Susannah and himself.

The Beginning of "Mother Love"

During your first trimester, you will start to know your baby in the most intimate of ways. One of nature's great riddles is how a mother can have such a deep relationship with her child before she has ever met or held that child. To this day, most people don't understand why women who miscarry early in their pregnancies experience overwhelming grief.

After this loss, even when they go on to have two or four or eight more children, they never forget the baby that they miscarried. Why? I believe it is because, from the first moment of conception, the mother-child connection is so profound, so biologically and emotionally and spiritually intense, that nothing on Earth can separate it.

Nearly 100 years ago, Sigmund Freud declared that "anatomy is destiny." Since then, many scholars, while appreciating the stilted Victorian era and European background from which his opinions derived, have resented Freud's sexist biases, believing they limited women's possibilities in the larger arenas of commerce, politics, the sciences, the arts, and industry.

But if Freud's reference to anatomy was, in fact, to female hormones, he was certainly right. As long as estrogen and progesterone course through every cell of the female body, women will always have that connection with their children. Notwithstanding the vital contribution of men in perpetuating the human race, it is still women who ovulate, menstruate, conceive, and, most significantly, carry and give birth to children. And it is this carrying, especially, this awe-inspiring act of sustaining a developing baby's life, that accounts for the ferocity of maternal passion.

And so it is with joy, and also a degree of anxiety, that mothers-to-be learn that they're pregnant and enter their fulfilling first trimester. Of course, their joy—even if it is tinged with ambivalence—is easy to understand, but what about the anxiety? Actually, this, too, is easy to appreciate if you think about anything that you have ever done for the first time or anything for which the outcome was unknown.

Having Faith in the Unknown

Even things that we have done thousands upon thousands of times, such as driving a car, carry with them the fear of the unknown. We have confidence in our own ability, but what about all the other drivers on the road? Or taking a qualifying exam; after all, we may have studied for the subject and received great grades in it, but the outcome of this particular test is unknown. How much greater, then, are the unknown factors in pregnancy, a process that is literally steeped in mystery?

Today, we are infinitely more informed than in the past. Yet, modern pregnancy involves so many tests and caveats that it has become, if anything, more anxiety-producing than it was in the good old days of ignorance.

For both former generations and this one, the existential questions remain the same: Will I be okay? Will my baby be healthy? Will things go well? Only an all-knowing God has the answers to these questions and that is why faith in God's wisdom is so important at this time.

This is not to suggest that you should not seek answers from other sources, primary among them your doctor or midwife. If you have been hesitant in the past about asking questions, this is the time to ask away. Don't forget: Your emotional well-being is as important to your developing baby as is anything else, so now is not the time to wonder and worry and let your imagination run away with troublesome doubts. Knowledge is power. Learning the answers to your questions will calm you, satisfy your intellectual curiosity, and equip you to take the proper steps.

Especially if you are having your first baby, you will want to know everything. And why shouldn't you? This is your body and your baby and the most important event of your life. If investigative reporters have no qualms about probing the President of the United States, then you—who is carrying the most important person in the world—should not hesitate to query any person or delve into any subject that may shed light on the many pressing issues that pregnancy presents.

Living in the Present

Once you learn that you're pregnant, your life becomes a marathon of planning for the future. As each day brings you closer to the due date—and in modern life, time elapses so quickly that even nine months seem to fly by with alarming speed—you're consumed with planning doctors' appointments, buying maternity clothes, seeking out child-care arrangements, shopping for a crib and a stroller, and also fulfilling impressive career and family responsibilities.

In the busyness of life, you may be so preoccupied with future events that it may seem easy to forget that life itself is not a dress rehearsal, that one's days are not practice sessions for some grand future event, but individual and precious moments that must be lived to the hilt.

While all of us may reminisce about (or idealize or agonize about) the past or fantasize about (or anticipate or dread) the future, the past is gone and the future unknown. The only time—the only seconds—that we can count on to live and feel and experience our lives is right now.

What an opportunity to reinvent those parts of yourself that you may have resolved to change before you became pregnant but never seemed to find the time for. What an ideal occasion to connect or reconnect with the spiritual part of yourself that you may have ignored in the past.

Making spiritual awareness a daily practice should be both pleasurable and easy, especially when you consider what incredible events are taking place inside you. For instance, at the moment you learn that you are pregnant, your baby's heart is already beating. Yes, within six weeks of conception, this tiny being has already developed an entire cardiovascular system with a heart that pumps blood with the same regularity, only twice as fast, as your own.

This astounding occurrence is only one of countless other wonders that are taking place outside your awareness, but only possible because of the internal environment that you are providing.

Your Baby's Sheltering Environment

Before making his or her grand entrance into the world, your baby spends nine months developing and growing larger in the protective confines of your womb. For between 36 and 40 weeks, your baby nestles in this sheltering environment, bathed in warm, nutritious fluid that also serves as a shock absorber for the normal bumps and jostles of pregnancy.

As even more protection against harm, your baby lies surrounded by the bony structure of your pelvis. During this time, according to an increasing body of persuasive research, your baby hears both soothing and jarring sounds and feels both pleasure and pain. Ultimately, your little one will enter the universe as the repository of all these prebirth experiences. This can be encouraging or daunting.

If a mother eats great quantities of french fries and hot dogs while she is pregnant, her unborn child receives every bit of the fat, cholesterol, and grease that she consumes. And if a mother smokes a pack a day during her pregnancy, her baby will receive all of the nicotine, tar, and other toxic chemicals that she inhales. Healthy habits are required for a healthy baby before, during, and after pregnancy.

Emotionally, things are quite the same. Flowing through the mother-to-be, directly into her developing baby, are surging hormones of serenity and stress. If a pregnant woman experiences the soothing effects of a gentle voice, a caring touch, a lilting tune, a word of reassurance, then her baby will benefit from these things in the same way she does. Conversely, if she is assailed by environmental or emotional harshness and responds as all people do to these assaults by manufacturing high levels of stress hormones, these, too, will find their way to her baby. So what's a mother-to-be to do? A lot.

Just as diets can be altered and smoking can be stopped, emotions, too, can be positively affected by a number of mood-altering influences. Certainly, love and support are two such influences as are music, a good experience, or even the passage of time. Others exist as well.

In transcendental meditation, the definition of the mantra that is repeated during the meditative process is "a word whose meaning is known." This brings about such a beneficial effect on the nervous system that it changes the galvanic skin response, lowers blood pressure, regulates irregular heartbeats, and brings about the deepest state of relaxation.

Spirituality affects every cell of a person's body, every neuron in the nervous system, every attitude, and every feeling. If you haven't already begun your spiritual childbirth journey, learning that you're pregnant presents yet another opportunity to begin. Here is an exercise that you and your partner can do not only at this very moment but also every day for the next nine months.

First, find a comfortable spot and sit down. Hold each other's hands—or better, place them on the new mother-to-be's lower abdomen, right over your baby's new "home." Then, close your eyes and take a long, quiet moment to collect your feelings and thoughts. Once you're comfortable, take two or three long, deep breaths, inhaling deeply to fill your lungs with the oxygen that will travel to and cleanse every cell of your body.

As you inhale, imagine yourself in a beautiful place on a beautiful day—the beach perhaps, or a park, or a mountaintop. As the air enters your system, picture yourself in that pristine setting and feel its purity entering your body. And every time you exhale, picture all the tension or anxiety or negative thinking that resides within you—the lightning bolts or piercing thorns or screeching sirens of emotional angst—being released into the atmosphere, never to return to your body again.

Now is a lovely time to revisit the here-and-now exercises that you began in chapter 2. Alone, or with your partner, take up the napkin once again, unfolding it with a renewed awareness of its qualities and a renewed appreciation of the abilities that you bring to this act.

Once again, focus on little things—the errant ant making its way across your floor, the pattern of your wallpaper, the ticking of your clock. In all of these acts, practice mindfulness, bringing to the individual moments of your life an understanding of their importance.

When you and your partner find yourselves rooted in the present, acutely aware of this very moment, you will be astoundingly appreciative of the miracle of your own and your baby's lives. What a perfect time to thank God for blessing you with a new life. Ask for the wisdom to do the right thing during your pregnancy—not only what is physically healthy but emotionally and spiritually nurturing to your baby and to each other as well.

Because an unforeseeable future lies before you, this is also the time to hope that you possess the insight and perspective to appreciate the very few months of your pregnancy for the gift they are. And last—because both present and future will be enhanced by your faith in God—now is another time to pray that your baby's journey will be safe and easy.

Chapter Ten

Your Fulfilling First Trimester
Invisible Miracles

All of us have listened to the music created by an orchestra or some other musical ensemble. Whether you heard the soaring works of Rachmaninoff or Beethoven, the seamless riffs of cool jazz, the driving rhythms of hard rock, or the emotionally charged highs and lows of country, chances are you felt the music deeply but hardly gave a thought to the many elements that went into producing it.

Where does music come from? How is it first expressed? What secret sources initially attract a musical person to the piano or the trombone or the harp or the cello? Scientists are just now looking into the hidden areas of the brain where the answers to these questions may lie, while musicians and composers seek the same answers in their hearts. All would agree, I think, that fathoming the orchestration of a human being is far more elusive.

That elusiveness was expressed most perfectly in Ecclesiastes: "As thou knowest not what is the way of the spirit, nor how the bones do grow in the womb of her that is with child: even so thou knowest not the works of God who maketh all." No, it is not—it cannot be—our job to understand the "breath of wind," that spirit of life that accounts for the mystery of childbirth.

But as you seek out the best prenatal care, read everything you can get your hands on, eat more wisely than you ever have before, and prepare yourself psychologically and spiritually for the challenge of parenthood, it is certainly exciting, indeed compelling, to learn of the wonderful things taking place inside you.

As your first trimester begins, you and your developing baby will undergo profound changes. Well before you realize that you're pregnant, your uterine lining—that cushiony bed that has received your embryo—continues to grow thicker. At the same time, a fluid-filled space with a smooth, glistening lining called the amnion develops around the embryo. This is commonly called the bag—and the fluid, the waters; hence, the bag of waters that will keep your baby safe, in an even temperature, cushioned against possible injury, and able to move about.

As your pregnancy progresses, you will experience various signs and symptoms and a changing shape, but at this point in early pregnancy, truly spectacular things are at work. While you can feel and see many of the changes, a million invisible processes are taking place outside your awareness.

Like an athlete preparing for a decathlon contest, your body is getting ready for an Olympic event. Just as your baby's embryonic systems are developing, your already-developed systems—neurological, digestive, cardiovascular, hormonal, all of them—are revving up to do the Herculean job of keeping not one, but two, people in the best of shape and the best of health. As Eric said, "Healthy trees, healthy apples."

A Tiny Being Starts to Grow

Among the most remarkable processes is the development of the three types of cells that will evolve into your baby's distinctive characteristics. From the beginning of development and throughout the first several months, the ectoderm cells will give rise to the skin, hair, nails, different types of glands, tooth enamel, and the nervous system.

The mesoderm cells will become muscle, bones, cartilage, tooth dentin, ligaments, tendons, kidneys, ureters, ovaries, testes, the heart, blood, lymph and blood vessels, and the linings of the heart, lungs, and abdominal cavities. And from the endoderm cells will arise the digestive tract, the lining of the respiratory tract, the bladder, the urethra, the thyroid gland, and the thymus.

All of these invisible processes occur while you go on busily living your life, unaware of the second-by-second miracles that are going on within you as you laugh at a joke, eat a meal, listen to a song, or sleep. But is lacking awareness of these processes the way it has to, or should be? Absolutely not. The point of spirituality is to make the recognition of these marvelous, life-giving processes never far from your awareness, never so remote that you fail to acknowledge the spirit that permeates every second of your experience.

For example, a routine habit like brushing one's teeth can now become a conscious act of taking care of oneself and, by association, one's developing infant. Calcium, the nutrient that, among others, accounts for healthy teeth, is commonly used by the developing baby. This is the time to make sure that your calcium intake is adequate and to have your teeth checked regularly by a dentist (sans x-rays).

What about the unconscious process of laughing at a joke? Studies have shown that laughter boosts the production of endorphins, chemical messengers in the brain known to elevate the mood. We already know that a mother's hormones are passed along to her embryo, so what a lovely gift to give your baby—good-mood hormones. Of course, eating a meal now becomes eating a nutritious meal, just as listening to a song soothes both your own and your developing baby's nervous system, and sleep rests the two of you as well.

Awareness of these unseen processes will enhance your life and make the early weeks of getting to know your little one a time of joy and true maternal attention. Your partner's interest in the fascinating inner workings of fetal development and pregnancy will be enhanced as well. When both of you take valued minutes together to contemplate these things and to marvel at the God responsible for creating life, your prayers for the continued harmony of your baby's development will flow effortlessly.

More Imperceptible Wonders

During the first four weeks of your pregnancy, not only does your tiny baby's heart begin to beat, propelling blood through microscopic arteries, but the entire foundation for the nervous and genitourinary and digestive systems begins to form, along with skin, bones, and lungs. In addition, the early beginnings of the eyes, ears, and nose appear, and budding arms and legs start to emerge. At less than a half-inch in length, the embryo's backbone is apparent and other systems are well underway. All this in four weeks.

By the end of the fourth week of pregnancy, the umbilical cord and placenta have formed. The cord, which derives from the abdominal wall of the embryo, is attached to the mother's placenta, just as the placenta is attached to the wall of the uterus. A versatile organ, the placenta transfers the exchange of gases, transports nutrition, maintains temperature, excretes wastes, and produces hormones (including estrogen and progesterone, among others).

At the end of the fifth week, the embryo becomes a fetus. During this time, the hemispheres of its brain develop rapidly, as do the intestines. By the end of the eighth week, astounding development has taken place. Now, your baby has quadrupled in length and is a little more than 1½ inches long. Recognizable human characteristics are apparent—arms and legs, fingers, toes, elbows, knees, and an unmistakably human face.

By the end of the third month of pregnancy, the fetus is 3 to 6 inches long, and weighs approximately 1 ounce. While your baby's gender was determined at the moment of conception, it is only now that the sex organs are recognizable. At this time, organ systems rapidly develop, fingernails and toenails emerge, baby teeth appear, and the developing kidneys begin to produce small amounts of urine.

Now the baby may begin to move, but not so strenuously that the movements can be felt by the mother. As this trimester comes to a close, your baby has developed all the systems that he or she will need to live outside the uterus. Over the next six months, nature's task—with your help—is to help all the systems of this teeny-tiny being to mature.

Just thinking about all the growth and change and "becoming" of your developing baby can be breathtaking. If you were watching a science program, visualizing the same processes unfolding on the screen, you would no doubt be astonished at each new stage. You might even be somewhat exhausted, wondering how so much growth could possibly take place in so short a time and in such a tiny being. But you are no spectator to this event. And while your baby is growing and changing, you are, too, and the changes in you are no less amazing.

How Mom Is Changing

Like the blossoming of a rose captured through time-lapse photography, the fetus undergoes awe-inspiring growth and development during its first three months. These invisible miracles are aided and abetted by the simultaneous changes and adaptations taking place in you.

Many changes will be emotional. As your pregnancy becomes more real to you, as you begin to adjust to the prospect of parenthood, and as you reveal your new status to family and friends and see their beaming smiles and obvious delight, your own excitement will grow and more than offset the normal physical discomforts of early pregnancy.

In addition to a little weight gain (or even a little weight loss if you experience some nausea and vomiting), you may experience, as mentioned before, some fatigue, breast tenderness, low back pain, constipation, and frequent urination. These diminish as time goes by; they are simply your body's adaptation to the extraordinary changes required to sustain the life of the child that you are carrying.

About one in five women have some spotting or bleeding in early pregnancy. While this does not necessarily mean a possible miscarriage, it is a symptom that requires immediate medical attention. After getting additional bed rest, cutting down on exercise, and abstaining from intercourse, the bleeding often subsides and the remainder of the pregnancy goes well.

During this time, your metabolism speeds up, the better to increase your body's efficiency in nourishing your baby; your uterus enlarges to accommodate your little one's growth; the milk-producing glands in your breasts develop; your bones are adapting to postural changes that pregnancy demands; your skin may undergo changes in coloration; and, for the first six weeks, your ovaries secrete hormones to sustain the pregnancy, a job that will soon be taken over by the placenta.

Whew! But all of these changes, including the discomforts, will not diminish the thrill and enthusiasm of early pregnancy, the fantasies of what your little girl or boy may look like, or the wonder of knowing that you are the in process of bringing a new life into the world.

Again, this is a wonderful time to acknowledge the great gift of pregnancy and the ability of your body to sustain a human life. When you and your partner are snug in your spiritual space, taking the time to acknowledge the presence of God, you will derive great peace and strength from your prayers. Perhaps this prayer will remind you of the important things that you would like to remember every day:

Dear God,

Please help me to remember that I am doing your most important work on Earth—bringing a new and precious life into the world.

Help me, as I go through my daily life, to consider what is consequential in the larger scheme of things: love, health, honest work, and a belief in your wisdom.

Guide me in making intelligent choices about the things I eat and drink, the activities I engage in, the thoughts I think, and in choosing life-affirming and positive relationships.

Make me wise enough to forgo anything that may harm my own health or the health of the baby I am carrying.

Give me the wisdom to enhance my relationship with my partner, to understand his role as the father of our baby, and to celebrate the fact that we, together, are becoming parents.

Endow us with the ability to enjoy and appreciate every stage of our baby's prenatal development and to give all praise to you for the miracle of pregnancy.

Finally, provide us with the strength to meet any adversity or weather any difficulty that may come our way.

So don't forget to treat yourself with loving care and to appreciate that you are in the process of doing God's work on Earth. As you enter your satisfying second trimester, bring with you the physical, emotional, and spiritual lessons that you have learned over the past three months.

Chapter
Eleven

Your Satisfying Second Trimester
Heartbeats and Fantasies

As you enter your second trimester—the fourth, fifth, and sixth months of pregnancy—you may find yourself increasingly in tune with nature and amazed at its unerring way of creating balance. By the fourth month, for instance, just when a woman may become completely demoralized with the symptoms of morning sickness, or irritated by the discomforts of heartburn, or sick of getting up in the middle of the night to urinate, her body adjusts to the hormonal changes that have brought these symptoms about, and they vanish.

This is a wonderful stage of pregnancy, with new and exciting things happening to you and your baby every day. In the fourth month, although your baby is only 4 to 6 inches in length and weighs just 2 to 4 ounces, he or she has grown to the point that you can now place your hand on your lower abdomen and feel the bulge of your growing uterus.

You may not yet show, but you will certainly know that your little bundle—your very little bundle—is making incredible progress. The baby's gender is now clearly visible, the kidneys are secreting urine, the nasal septum and palate have closed, eyebrows have appeared, and a sonogram may show the baby sucking its thumb.

Ta-dums and Blips

It is during this month that one of the most thrilling events of pregnancy takes place—the first audible sounds of your baby's heartbeat, heard through either a fetoscope or monitoring machine. While most of the other processes of pregnancy are experienced by the mother-to-be alone, since it is she who is carrying the baby, the sound of that rhythmic ta-dum, ta-dum, is one experience both the mother-to-be and the father-to-be can share.

Many men genuinely empathize with their partner's experience, but until they hear the rhythmic beating of that heartbeat, their roles are of a spectator nature. Once both of you have heard the regular cadence of these thrilling pulsations, the reality of your own impending parenthood is reinforced, and you may now begin to look at other infants and children with renewed fascination.

The sound of your baby's heartbeat is a moment to celebrate and be thankful. It is another time when that spiritual space that you have established might be spent in prayerful gratitude and in a renewed appreciation of God's awesome power to give and sustain life.

By the end of your fifth month—more than halfway through your pregnancy—your baby will be approximately 12 inches in length and weigh about 1 pound. Hairs have begun to sprout on your little one's head, and the baby's entire body is now covered with a downy growth of fine hair called lanugo, which offers the skin protection from the surrounding fluid environment.

At this time another monumental milestone of pregnancy takes place when the mother-to-be feels an ever-so-slight, very hard-to-describe sensation. Blip. At first, it is so imperceptible that you may ignore it or even think that you are having a little indigestion. But shortly, that little blip feels more like a flutter. And then that flutter becomes, well, a more pronounced flutter. This truly thrilling sensation is called quickening, and all at once you'll know—this is your baby moving. Your little one has been moving about for some time now, but this will be your own first awareness of movement.

Nothing on Earth affects a woman more than feeling her baby move. While she may have thrilled to the sight of her baby on a sonogram and been ecstatic at the sound of the heartbeat, the sensation of movement is the moment when most women feel the first real passion of maternal empathy and love. This experience is so bonding, so emblematic of the intimacy of the mother-child relationship, and so inexpressibly profound that, for many women, it becomes the point in their pregnancies when they find themselves turning inward.

"I Don't Want to Know"

The emotional exhilaration that you may experience during pregnancy can be as high as the moon and the stars. But concealed deep within each woman's heart is the anxiety that her child may not be normal. That possibility haunts the modern woman, since those giving birth after the age of 35 are at higher risk for delivering children with birth defects.

Waiting to learn if the results of amniocenteses, alpha-fetoprotein tests, chorionic villi sampling, and ultrasound exams will reveal abnormalities is unbearably anxiety-producing. And the cruel thing about this kind of "progress" is that many of these tests are performed in the fourth and fifth months of pregnancy, when a woman's girth is enlarging, her fantasies of motherhood are flourishing, and she has already experienced those thrilling ta-dums and blips.

These tests can—and often do—mute the elation of the second trimester. While you will be eager to learn what direction your own life and your baby's life will take, you will no doubt join all the other people in the world who have taken "scary" tests and faced their results by crying, "I don't want to know."

In addition to causing emotional upheaval, testing for birth defects often stretches a woman and her partner to their moral and philosophical limits, forcing them to think about making one of two overwhelmingly difficult decisions: raising a seriously impaired child (or one who may be destined to die) or having an abortion. At this time, parents are called upon to "play God." The same issues arise when a child is born with overwhelming problems or dies at birth or shortly after. How could this happen?

Facing Harsh Realities

If you are going for these tests and they reveal that all is fine, you will remember that moment of relief forever. If they do not turn out well, you will be called upon to be wise and forebearing as never before. At no time will your relationship to each other and to God be more meaningful. At no time will prayer be more guiding. At no time will putting your faith in and trusting God's wisdom be more important.

And yet, just at the time when love and faith can be most healing, your relationship—and your faith in God—

may be sorely tested. It is one thing to read or even hear about life's slings and arrows, but quite a different thing to face them. When it comes to confronting harsh realities, there are no hard rules of conduct and no predicting how each person will react.

Some people fall apart, but recoup and then rise to the challenge before them. Others don't break stride, but suffer silently, often to the detriment of their own health. Some people look for someone—or something—to blame. Others reach out to learn from the hard-earned wisdom of others. If you should be faced with circumstances that seem too difficult to bear, perhaps the following guidelines will help.

Let Your Tears Flow

Poets speak of bitter tears, of drowning in tears, of the weeping of mothers into the night. In some cultures, grieving people shred their clothes; in others, they keen and wail in groups. In our culture overt expressions of emotions—especially sad ones—do not come easily, especially for men who are conditioned to be strong and hold things in.

But tears not only have a cleansing effect emotionally, they also rid the system of built-up toxins that accumulate when grief changes the body's chemistry. It's good to cry. When you're stunned, disappointed, bewildered, or hurt, when you don't know what to do or where to turn—crying is appropriate, understandable, and human.

Get Angry

In our culture anger has a bad name. Actually, it's one of our most powerful, useful, and effective emotions. If you notice the letters to the editor of any publication, the overwhelming majority express displeasure or downright anger at various issues. The writers of these letters have been mobilized by anger and have used it to address important subjects.

Some of the great social issues of our time have been addressed by people so angry at injustice that they have taken to the streets, lobbied elected officials, and ultimately brought about corrective legislation.

Beneath the anguish of heartache lies anger. Anger at life. Anger at fate. Anger at God. Remember Johanna in chapter 2, who screamed at God, "How could you do this to me? You're a fake"? I knew another woman who, like Johanna, had experienced great grief. When she told her priest how angry she was at God, he replied, "That's okay, God can take it."

So get angry. Like tears, the expression of anger cleanses the system. And often, it acts as a catalyst to important change.

Join a Support Group

All over the country, grassroots or community- and hospital-based support groups have proved to be lifesavers for people undergoing traumatic events. In such a group you will meet people who have "been there," gone through what you are going through, cried and shaken their fists at God, and finally resolved their anguish.

Often, people who join such groups find themselves helping others. Reaching into a wellspring of strength that they may have thought they lost, they find the wisdom and insight to help their suffering neighbor. And by so doing, they help themselves.

Seek Professional Help

Everyone has a different threshold for stress. In some people a traumatic event may lead to a reactive depression that runs its course and dissipates with time. Psychotherapy can be helpful in this case. For those who have a constitutional vulnerability, the same event may trigger a biological depression. Here, psychotherapy may be supportive, but medication will be needed to realign the chemical imbalance that has taken place. In any case, if depression is protracted, it's a good idea to seek professional help.

Trust in God

At a time of suffering and distress, you may feel betrayed, as Johanna did, by a God who you thought was benevolent. "Where was the kindness?" Johanna asked. Often it is impossible to fathom God's design, to comprehend the way the world works. At this time, you don't even have to look for reason. But over time, it will become known to you. As life goes on, as circumstances change, as your strength and optimism return, you will feel God's presence and you will know that he has shown you the way.

Moving Along

Before you know it, you will complete your second trimester. By this time, the end of your sixth month, your little one will be 12 to 14 inches in length and weigh about 2 pounds. The baby has now developed a protective fatty covering called vernix caseosa (literally, "cheesy varnish"). At this stage, the baby's eyes can open and he or she can hear.

Another amazing event now happens—your baby develops an identifying feature that not one of the more than six billion people on this planet shares: one-of-a-kind fingerprints. By this time, you feel real rib-jarring kicks from your little acrobat throughout the day and night.

Every time your baby moves and kicks is the perfect time to acknowledge the miracle of life, to express gratitude for your baby's vigor, to thank God for the privilege of carrying a baby within you, and to pray for continued health, well-being, and wisdom.

A More Beautiful You

Perhaps the most characteristic trait of a woman in her second trimester is that she radiates an incandescent glow. "Now that you're showing, you're glowing," one apt adage has it. Women themselves attest to this view, often saying that they feel more beautiful at this time than they ever have before.

Everything that is womanly, feminine, earthy, and bountiful now becomes manifest. The body is round and ripe. The skin is tinged with the blush of impending motherhood. The breasts are abundant and full. The gait is of modest pride. The fingers brush the abdomen with a nurturing caress. The face is a beatific Madonna's.

Wordlessly, your very presence now announces to the world, "I am with child." And the world—intimates and strangers alike—responds with unconditional joy and reverence.

You are no longer troubled by the unpleasant symptoms of early pregnancy. You have adjusted to the idea of motherhood. Your interest in sex has returned. Now, you are in full bloom—comfortable with your body, thrilled by the movements of your baby, sensual and sexy, and exulting in the changes that are taking place.

The most obvious change is in your shape. As your baby has been increasing in size, your waist has been slowly disappearing. One day, you will wake up to find it gone. The baby now occupies so much space that the top of your uterus is just above the umbilicus.

That's right—your baby, both figuratively and literally, is right under your heart. As your stomach enlarges, you may notice some stretch marks and a decrease in the effortless ease that you once had in moving around or in finding a comfortable sleeping position. There may be other bothersome changes at this time: increased allergies, backaches from your stretching muscles and ligaments, and perhaps the appearance of varicose veins in your legs.

But all these signs and symptoms of normal pregnancy usually don't gang up on you at one time, nor are they always present at the same time. God's orchestration of the various stages of pregnancy is another example of the perfect harmony of the universe.

While each stage has its discomforts and anxieties, they are inevitably accompanied by the flawless balance that anticipation and joy provide and by the knowledge that each characteristic sign is a preamble to life's greatest gift—a baby. While dealing with an even more beautiful you will be among the happiest experiences of your pregnancy, coping with some of the more bothersome signs and symptoms can test even the most stalwart of women.

Creating a Patchwork Quilt

A mother of six told me how she dealt with the discomforts of each of her pregnancies. Emma was a quilter and quite introspective by nature. When I entered her home, the first thing that I noticed was a saying from the Psalms that she had made in needlepoint: "For you created my inmost being; you knit me together in my mother's womb. I praise you because I am fearfully and wonderfully made; your works are wonderful, I know that full well."

I wasn't surprised that Emma utilized her spiritual nature in coping with six children. She told me that "creating a patchwork quilt is a metaphor for creating a life—they're really quite similar." While three of her adorable children scampered about, she spoke about the many elements that go into a quilt: the threads, the needles, the thimble, the scissors, the patches of fabric, the borders, the frame, the energy, and especially the inspiration.

"Deciding to do something you love, that's like choosing the right partner," she explained. "Then gathering the right tools, that's like eating a good diet and taking good care of yourself. And finding the pieces that will go together, that will blend with each other, that will become something beautiful, that's like all the elements that go into your baby, all the things you hope that God will fit together perfectly."

Emma said she always tried to look at the symptoms of her pregnancy as she looked at a quilting project. "I had morning sickness for four of my pregnancies, and most of the typical symptoms, like heartburn and fatigue, for all of them," she said. "Whenever I felt bad, I would remind myself of making a quilt—the tedious part of going over stitches, the bleary eyes when I had a project due, the times I'd stick myself so often that my fingers looked like little pin cushions. I just knew that nothing wonderful comes to you without at least a little difficulty. So whenever I woke up feeling nauseated, the first thing I did was pat my stomach and say to myself, 'This is going to be a beautiful creation.'"

By using her quilting experience as a guide, Emma was even creative in the way she dealt with her nausea. She converted this unpleasant symptom, as she did others, into an affirmation. She perceived the symptom as a harbinger of good things to come, seeing it as part and parcel of a complicated process that involved "a little difficulty" and also wonder. This way of coping with the inevitable discomforts of pregnancy is available to everyone. And the wonderful thing about it is that using your imagination and resolve to see the whole picture— the whole quilt—can be summoned up at will.

A quilting view of things, or any view that grants you perspective and hope, will help you through all the changes that you're experiencing, from physical annoyances to up-and-down moods to feeling more stress at work. But don't stop there. Now is the time to call upon everything that is available to you.

Even if you're not athletic and have never jogged or taken an aerobics class, exercise that is less demanding can now help you to deal with many of pregnancy's discomforts. Swimming, biking, walking—all are wonderful exercises that will get you away from it all, clear your mind, stimulate those happy hormones, and make you feel good all over. Just check with your doctor before undertaking anything new to make sure it's right for you.

And speaking of exercise, in only four to five weeks you will probably be signing up for a prepared-childbirth course. In addition to learning breathing exercises, you will be learning pelvic floor and abdominal muscle exercises that will strengthen the muscles most strained by pregnancy. Don't wait until then. Ask your doctor or midwife to recommend a childbirth teacher who will teach you these exercises now. They will make you feel good and will help to ease the muscle strain of late pregnancy.

One warning here: During any stage of pregnancy, don't ignore potential danger signals such as any bleeding, abdominal pain, swelling of the face and fingers, a change in your baby's movements, or a severe headache. If any of these appear, seek medical attention immediately.

Dreams and Fantasies

During your second trimester, your fantasies and dreams may take on more color. As you discuss possible names, you may imagine that this vigorous little creature will be an athlete or a dancer, a night owl or a morning lark. And, of course, you'll be superstitious as well, not wanting to do or say or even think anything that might bode poorly.

You are now two-thirds through your pregnancy and about to enter the homestretch—your third trimester. Busier than ever and experiencing dramatic changes in your shape and feelings every day, it is important for you to stay in touch with the spiritual realm of your pregnancy. Pay attention to what your dreams and fantasies are telling you. Write them down and keep track of what they mean to you. In the coming months, as you feel closer to your baby and to God, you will draw on them and all that has gone before to help you navigate the last mile of pregnancy.

It's Not Always Easy to Think Spiritually

While you may nod in assent and resolve to feel the presence of God in all that is transpiring, I am aware that for most people it is very difficult, if not impossible, to factor spiritual thinking into daily life.

For one thing, it is somewhat scary. After all, if one thinks constantly of the invisible processes that are involved in conception and pregnancy, one might go about on tiptoes, afraid to upset the delicate balance of nature. In addition, it is not always easy to take that deep breath, find that deeper meaning, or reflect on the events that are swirling about you.

And yet, most people yearn to seize the day, to appreciate the wonder of beginning life, to think about ordinary things in a new and life-affirming way. In some cultures, spiritual thinking is so much a part of daily life that nobody considers it extraordinary. Inevitably, however, the more hectic life becomes, the more difficult it is to tap one's spiritual center and to experience the benefits that derive from this rich source of wisdom. Please know that there are many ways to connect with your inner spirit.

Watching the Birds

A few years ago, I met a woman whose name, appropriately, was Joy. Joy told me that the lessons she had learned from her first pregnancy had led her to have a more "joyful and spiritual" second pregnancy.

"Ever since I was a little girl," she said, "I was a serious person, always trying to figure out the meaning of the universe, always asking 'why?' So when I became pregnant with my first child, all I could think about was the meaning of life and the importance of my role in carrying my child. I was so grateful to be having a baby and so thankful to God, but I didn't seem to feel the joy of the whole thing, and I didn't know why. There it is again—why? why? why?"

When Joy's little son was two years old, she and her husband moved from a city apartment to a house in the suburbs, and she became pregnant with her second child. At a housewarming party, one of her friends brought her a most original gift—a bird-feeder, a six-month supply of bird food, and a book to help the novice bird-watcher identify each species.

Joy hung the feeder outside her kitchen window and watched as the birds began to swoop and flutter and balance themselves with perfect precision on the multi-tiered contraption. Pretty soon, she found herself consulting the bird guide, shrieking with delight as she identified the softly cooing mourning doves, the raspberry-dipped purple finches, the bright red cardinals, the sassy blue jays, and the titmice, sparrows, and chickadees. One day, when she saw a red-bellied woodpecker for the first time, she got so excited that she called her husband at work.

"I was so enthralled with my birds," she told me, "that I found myself spending half of my day just thinking about how amazing they were, how they perched with perfect balance on the branches and took turns at the feeder, how their colors changed from winter to spring, how they knew when I put out a new batch of food. I wondered where they slept at night and laughed out loud to myself when I occasionally caught sight of their adorable babies."

Joy told me that when she was by herself, watching the birds, she realized more keenly than ever how miraculous the universe was, how fragile yet strong life was, and especially how much a part of nature her own experience of being pregnant was.

"I loved that pregnancy," she said, "because I stopped thinking about myself so much. Somehow, watching my birds was a spiritual experience, and it made me able to feel spiritual about my own little fledgling."

It is significant that Joy's insight came from being by herself. While turning toward the self is a universal experience for pregnant women, it is rarely considered a crucial part of the process of becoming a mother.

While we spend years in school preparing ourselves for independent life, women have only nine months to prepare for a job that has no guidelines, no paradigms, and no instructions. There is a lot to think about, to wonder about, even to worry about, and so women, with their unparalleled intuition and instinct for survival, turn to themselves and to their God-given wisdom.

That instinct often inspires women to engage in a quiet, focused activity like quilting or to find meaning in watching the birds outside their windows. During the last weeks of the second trimester, many women gravitate naturally toward some form of quiet meditation.

As you contemplate entering your last trimester, you may find yourself seeking out more often that quiet corner that you have established, looking forward to entering the spiritual space that you have been sharing with your partner, spending more quiet time with your thoughts, and praying for continued health and strength.

This is a lovely time to speak to your baby about your future together, to use your powers of visualization to picture the features on your baby's face, the shock of hair, the soft, downy skin. Try to see the opening and closing of your baby's tiny hands, the flexing of dimpled knees, the curling of "little piggy" toes, the blinking of sleepy eyelids.

Is your little one kicking up a storm? Can't you just picture your baby using those sturdy legs to jump on your lap, kick a ball, or dance around the room? Is your little one quiet now? As you imagine this perfect being, curled up and slumbering peacefully within you, what a beautiful time for you to croon a soothing lullaby.

Chapter Twelve

Turning Inward
The Need for Emotional Solitude

At the same time a woman feels herself becoming closer to her unborn baby, she may be growing more dreamy and less accessible to others. It is as though she is saying to the world, "This is the beginning of a precious relationship, and I need time to think about it, to feel about it, and to pay attention to both my baby and myself."

It is quite common, in fact, for mothers-to-be to become moody and self-preoccupied during the second trimester. More sensitive to the reality of the new life stirring within them, they may also feel overwhelmed by the prospect of motherhood and, as a result, increasingly dependent. Often, this is the time that a woman reflects on her relationship with her own mother and begins to question if she will be able to be a good mother herself.

If she has enjoyed a loving relationship with her mother, she is bound to feel confident about her own role. There are legions of women, however, who have had less-than-optimal relationships with their mothers. During pregnancy, the problems caused by their relationships may loom large, causing the mother-to-be to be riddled with self-doubt. This is certainly a time when women need to ask for extra love and reassurance from the people who are closest to them.

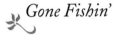 *Gone Fishin'*

Elizabeth was in her early thirties when she became pregnant for the first time. A beautiful woman with a captivating personality, she designed magnificent jewelry and handbags for a prominent firm in New York City. Married to a successful (and dashing) lawyer, she appeared to her friends to have it all. Elizabeth believed this, too, until she got pregnant and became deeply depressed.

After a few sessions with a psychotherapist, Elizabeth realized that unresolved conflicts with her mother were at the root of her depression. "Whatever I do or ever did," she said, "my mother criticized it, and I ended up feeling like it wasn't enough, that I was supposed to try harder to be—I don't know what— better."

When she joyfully announced her pregnancy, her mother had only one response: "Say good-bye to your figure." When she told her that the baby's middle name would be in honor of her, her mother said, "First is an honor, middle is nothing." Elizabeth's stories went on and on, each of them detailing an entire history of her mother's negativity and her own efforts to be "better." Although Elizabeth had a loving husband and several close friends, she continued to feel an urgent need for her mother's approval.

Over and over, she told the psychotherapist, "I want

to be a good mother, but I just know that history will repeat itself. I'm afraid of treating my own baby the way my mother treats me."

When Elizabeth was in her third month, her husband, Austin, thought that taking a vacation to Martha's Vineyard, where they had honeymooned, would cheer her up. For the first time in their lives, they decided to go fishing for trout and rented the equipment at a nearby dock. Casting their lines, they were delighted to be reeling in fish within an hour. But no trout.

After they had thrown all their catches back in the water, Elizabeth's line became tangled, and they decided to call it quits. But, a nearby fisherman offered to help untie the line and, quite by chance, helped lift her depression. As he worked, Elizabeth tried to make small talk. "It's such a nice day," she said, "but my husband and I aren't having any luck. We've caught a lot of fish, but not what we came here to catch. I guess the trout aren't swimming today."

At that, the fisherman threw back his head and, to Elizabeth's bewilderment, laughed and laughed and laughed. "That's a good one," he chortled. "Of course, you didn't catch trout. This is the ocean and trout don't swim in the ocean. Flounder, tuna, mackerel, you name it—but not trout. If you want to catch trout, you've got to fish in a stream. The problem is, young lady, you've been fishin' in the wrong waters."

"Oh my goodness," Elizabeth cried to Austin, "we've been fishing in the wrong waters." Both of them laughed all the way back to their hotel, but those words kept going around and around in Elizabeth's head, and they stayed with her all the way back to New York.

A couple of days later, she was in her studio applying the finishing touches to a beaded bag when she stopped cold. In a moment of epiphany, she realized that in seeking approval from her mother, she was looking for

*trout in the ocean. "I've been fishing in the wrong
waters," she exclaimed to an astonished colleague.*

*With that insight, Elizabeth reinvented herself. It
wasn't long before she lost her fear of history repeating
itself. "My mother brought her own history to
motherhood," she proclaimed one day, "and I'll bring my
own as well, not hers."*

*Turning inward and using the laws of nature as a
guide, Elizabeth looked deeply at an issue that she had
avoided her whole life and resolved it to the benefit of
herself and her child.*

Narcissism—Not at All

Unfortunately, modern psychology has labeled this
turning inward narcissistic. In this age, narcissism con-
notes a somewhat unhealthy self-involvement, a preoccu-
pation with oneself that is not beneficial or even realistic.
It is important to remember here that most theorists have
been men, and even the most sympathetic and qualified
among them has never been pregnant.

It is far more accurate to view the self-involvement of
women in their second trimesters as a reaction to the overwhelming awareness—catalyzed by their enlarging girths
and the fluttering movements of their developing babies—
that, yes, life is here, life is within me, and I am responsible
for this life. So enormous is this realization, so breathtaking, that it literally eclipses all other considerations.

Before this time, the advent of motherhood is somewhat abstract. The missed period is exciting, anxiety-producing, and, if the pregnancy test is positive, thrilling.
Early symptoms of pregnancy, even nausea and vomiting,
make the diagnosis even more real. And a little weight
gain and some subtle signs of a changing shape add to the
reality of pregnancy. But these do not compare to the first

real stirrings of life or to the maternal empathy and love they engender. And that is not all.

It is at this moment when most women begin to realize that only a few months lie ahead before they will give birth. Before this, women are appropriately concerned with their own health and, intellectually, with their child's. But with the first sensation of life inside them, they realize that more is at work in the grand scheme of things than simply doing the right thing.

Now that she has felt her baby moving about, this issue is no longer theoretical. She feels loving and protective of the tiny human being inside her but, at the same time, aware that even if she does everything right, the yearned-for health of her child is not guaranteed. This is a sobering, even frightening, realization.

Here, we live our lives trying to maintain some semblance of control, only to find that when it comes to the most important issues, we are not in control. No wonder we turn inward at this time. And how significant. Turning inward means turning to our spiritual center. Although this act may not be consciously recognized, it is truly an instinctive response, a tacit acknowledgment that answers to our questions and anxieties lie deep within us, as do both God and baby.

Most of the women that I've met have never mentioned the word *spiritual*. But all of them, in thinking and feeling about their own safety through childbirth and their baby's health, implicitly accepted that, beyond their own power and beyond their doctor's or midwife's power, there was another power, a power so immense that it alone—God alone—held the keys.

That is why, rather than narcissistic, I call the self-pre-occupation of women in the second trimester appropriate and healthy. After all, there is no architect who ever designed a building, no artist who ever created a symphony or an oil painting or a poem, no business person who ever created a multimillion-dollar firm, no astronaut who ever landed on the moon, no philanthropist who ever benefited the world, no doctor who ever saved a life, and no scientist who ever discovered a cure whose accomplishments could compare with the creation of a life.

Some women may conceal their anxieties or speak about them with trusted friends. Both of these strategies can be helpful. Repression in the service of peace of mind is often an intuitively healthy response, and speaking with an empathic person can be equally, if not more, helpful.

Also speak to God, who knows and understands everything, especially those things that mere mortals can only guess at or hope for or imagine. One of the most peaceful and earthy women I've ever met described her spiritual journey through pregnancy and childbirth.

Learning Life's Great Lessons

For many years Edie had been an operating-room nurse with a specialty in open-heart surgery. From this vantage point she participated in the great dramas of life and death and witnessed the crashing despair and life-affirming optimism that accompany critical health conditions. She told me that of the hundreds of patients she had spoken to before surgery, then scrubbed for during surgery, then followed up after surgery, "no two were alike, except in one way."

"Everyone is nervous before such surgery," Edie explained, "but in every single case, the patients who believed in God, who had some spiritual core, were more at peace and seemed to fare better." She acknowledged that her observations were "not scientific," but "if anyone ever does a study, there is no doubt in my mind that what I saw time and again, year after year, will prove true."

Edie told me that her years as a nurse influenced her deeply when she became pregnant for the first time. "I wanted to learn from my patients," she said. "I wanted to feel the inner strength they felt and know as they did that a force larger than myself was with me. After all, except for having a baby, when do people face their own mortality more than when a doctor opens a chest and actually handles the very essence of what it means to be a person, a human heart?"

From the moment she learned that she was pregnant, Edie said that she felt "at peace with the universe." She explained, "I knew how fragile my little embryo was and I often wondered if everything was progressing as it should and if it would turn out all right. But every time I felt even a little bit nervous, I would sit down in a quiet place and think about God's wisdom and say a little prayer."

Edie did the same through four pregnancies, three of them uncomplicated, one with several problems. "I knew that problems were part of life," she said. "I certainly saw that in the operating room." She told me, however, that the same comfort she felt from tapping into her spiritual center during her pregnancies also helped her cope with the problems that arose. "That's the secret," she said. "God is also the source of all strength."

When the Father-to-Be Feels Left Out

For many women, it takes another kind of strength to cope with relationship changes that may take place during the second trimester, particularly the relationship with their partners. One result of the turning inward that occurs is that it is so frequently misinterpreted.

This is understandable. For a man, his partner's pregnancy is a highly personal, exciting, and somewhat nerve-wracking event—he is about to become a father. On the other hand, he can only observe or try to understand all the changes taking place. As his partner turns her attention to herself and to the tiny life that is growing inside her, the father-to-be may feel displaced, as Tony in chapter 9 did at the beginning of his wife's pregnancy. Where once he may have been the sole focus of his partner's attention, he may now feel ignored and neglected. Rationally, he may know that his partner's turning inward is a transitory phenomenon, but rationality does not always prevail.

> For example, Anne-Marie and Nick, a couple attending one of my Lamaze courses, had been married for seven years before they decided to have a baby. During those years, they had worked together to build a thriving public relations business—she, the graphic artist and wordsmith; he, the sales and marketing guru.
>
> During the first class I noticed that everything Anne-Marie said, Nick commented about in a somewhat facetious way. Although I wouldn't say that they had "bad vibes," they certainly lacked the kind of cozy warmth that the other couples shared. The second class was the same, with Nick describing Anne-Marie as "too obsessed with having the baby."
>
> Just before the third class, Anne-Marie called me, tearful and bewildered. She told me that she and Nick had been college sweethearts and madly in love until, that is, "I became pregnant, and all of a sudden, he seemed to change." She wanted me to know that they "really loved each other" and that "the Nick you're seeing in your classes is not the 'real' Nick that has always supported me through everything."
>
> They agreed to come an hour early for the third class, where I had the chance to speak with Nick. He confirmed everything that Anne-Marie had told me on the phone. Yes, he was still madly in love with her and

supported her in every way. He said that the four years of their courtship and seven years of their marriage had made him feel "like a king every day," but that since Anne-Marie had become pregnant, "I'm definitely not number one anymore." I felt the poignancy of his words.

When Anne-Marie heard Nick verbalize his feelings, she understood why he had changed, that his behavior was a result of his fear of being replaced in her affections by their baby. And when she explained to him how overwhelmed she felt by the prospect of juggling motherhood, being a wife, and keeping up with her job, Nick appreciated why she had become "obsessed."

Happily, this 20-minute exchange went a long way in clarifying almost nine months of misunderstanding. And none too soon. Anne-Marie went into labor three weeks early, with Nick lovingly by her side and no longer afraid that the life they had created together was in any way a threat to him or his place in Anne-Marie's affections.

An atmosphere sparkling with clarity, hope, and love provides the optimal environment for a harmonious pregnancy. Too many wonderful things take place, practically every minute, to waste precious time misunderstanding one another. Never will your relationship be more important than when you enter your third and last trimester.

Chapter Thirteen

Entering Your Third Trimester

Having Fun and Fighting Fear

All at once, six months have flown by, and you have entered the last trimester of your pregnancy, with each day bringing new and dramatic changes to both you and your baby. This is also a time—a mere 12 weeks from delivery—when many pleasurable activities take on added timeliness.

You may now be the star of a baby shower at which your family, friends, and coworkers lavish you with gifts, plenty of advice, and tales of their own experiences of childbirth. If it's not a surprise shower, you may have the opportunity to tell people what things you need. If it is a surprise, enjoy it.

But not everyone has a shower thrown for them. Maybe you just moved to a new location and haven't yet established any new relationships, or you may be a person with only one or two good friends. These circumstances should not discourage you from throwing yourself a shower. One of the wonderful things about embracing a spiritual dimension into your life is the opportunity it offers to think twice about everything, to reinvent yourself as Elizabeth in chapter 12 did when she discovered that she was fishing in the wrong waters.

> *Justine did just that. A self-described loner who spent her days peering into a microscope at a research institute in California, Justine told me, "I got as much pleasure from searching for viruses and their mutations as someone else might get from performing on Broadway." She and her husband, Tom, another passionate researcher, left their jobs each day to return to an authentic log cabin, which they had built with their own hands on a remote plot of land an hour's drive from the research lab. "I can honestly say that we had no friends," she said quite merrily, "which was fine with us, since we were each other's best friends."*
>
> *When Justine learned that she was pregnant, she and Tom were deliriously happy and everything went well until her eighth month, when she began to feel lonely and "sort of not connected to anyone." Her family was in France, and Tom's family, to whom they were not particularly close, was scattered throughout the country. "All of a sudden," she said, "I wanted to be just a typical person and to have, of all things, a baby shower." At first, she said, she felt sad and wondered if being such a solitary person was the right thing to be.*
>
> *One evening, she was speaking with Tom about her research. "I was telling him how elusive these little viruses were, that they just had a life of their own. And*

then it came to me—if these microscopic, invisible little creatures can be so independent, then certainly I can."
Not knowing how to be typical, Justine went to the library and looked up "baby showers."

"You should have seen our cabin," she exclaimed with glowing pride. "I hung streamers and balloons around the room and on the front door. I set the table with a tablecloth and candles. I cooked some delicious dishes. And I went out and bought all the things the baby would need and wrapped them in gift paper. I even put different-colored bows and ribbons on them. Then Tom and I called our midwife and a couple of people from the lab, and I had the greatest baby shower in the world."

Interestingly, Justine's inspiration, like Elizabeth's and that of so many others, had come from nature—in her case, those infinitesimal viruses that had a life of their own. Instead of waiting for someone to give her what she wanted and needed, she opened herself up to the lessons of nature by concentrating on little things, just as Rena in chapter 2 had when she made a study of butterfly wings. Then, tapping into her own resourcefulness, Justine provided herself with the perfect baby shower.

Advice and War Stories

While mostly well-intentioned, advice is by its nature subjective. Even in the same family, no two children are ever brought up in the same way. Circumstances change, parents change, relationships change, wisdom itself changes, and each child is such a unique amalgam of his own emotions, intellect, talents, or limitations that "formulas" that may work very well for one may be inappropriate or even counterproductive for another.

Practical advice, however, may be invaluable. For instance, if you live in a big house where your new baby's bedroom is distant from your own, getting an intercom to listen for baby's cries or coughs or crankiness can save many steps and much anxiety. But advice that derives from the emotions is acquired through experience alone and is therefore very individual.

One mother may tell you, for example, that breast-feeding is an absolute prerequisite for bonding with your new baby. This popular notion has unfortunately produced unnecessary guilt in mothers who either don't want to breast-feed or, for some medical reason, cannot. In fact, vast populations of people have lived and continue to live long, healthy lives without having been breast-fed, just as mothers who bottle-feed have proved to be as loving and devoted and maternal as those who breast-feed.

You alone are the best one to make this decision, and both you and your partner are the best ones to decide how to live your lives and raise your child. So, when it comes to taking advice, keep those grains of salt on hand.

As for those war stories that you hear from women who have already given birth, you may have to get some cotton for your ears and a handful of that salt. Because we humans are a very quirky bunch, we seem never to tire of repeating the most gruesome or frightening aspects of our experiences. Perhaps it is because we are so relieved to have lived through them, there is a particular delight or need to describe the thunder, the lightning, the downpour.

In literally thousands of births I attended as a delivery-room R.N., the overwhelming majority did not involve the 40-hour labors that you will hear about or any other frightful stories. So keep your ears open for all of the affirmative stories that exist and, if you should hear a horror story, simply ask that person, "Why are you telling me this? Do you think it will be helpful to me when I go into labor?"

What's in a Name?

Among the other fun things that you'll be thinking about and discussing in your last trimester is your baby's name—unless, that is, you had decided early that your baby, if a boy, will be a Junior or a third, or that he or she will have the name of a relative.

Poring through name books, trying out this or that name with your last name, "test-marketing" your tentative choices on friends and family, and letting your imagination picture what Alexis or Savannah or Tyler or Matthew may look like or be like—all can make the choosing of a name creative and fun.

But what if there is a conflict—you absolutely hate the name your partner loves or vice versa? Some couples resolve such conflicts by taking turns—she chooses the name of the first child, he the second. Others find at least a few names that are, if not thrilling to both of them, at least satisfactory. And, of course, there are cases in which this issue is never resolved, and the ultimate choice makes one parent unhappy.

Not a frivolous issue, your baby's name is who he or she is, the identifying moniker that will be presented to the world hundreds of thousand of times throughout life. Will it be euphonious with your last name? Will it lend itself to ridicule? Will it be abbreviated into a satisfactory nickname? Will it be a name associated in your mind with someone, either living or deceased, who is not held in affection?

When children are named for a disliked relative, or one who is remembered for his oddness or criminal past or meanness of spirit, those memories will color your own perceptions and even shape any future criticisms. Your child, no doubt, will one day develop individual quirks or foibles, qualities that may inspire your comment or criticism. But in choosing a name that is free of negative or painful associations, you will make sure that he or she never hears those dismal, accusatory words, "You're just like so-and-so." Sometimes, waiting until after the baby is born is the best course of action.

> Janine had always loved the name Tina. Her childhood best friend, a petite and graceful brunette, had been named Tina, and Janine held that image in her mind whenever she thought of the name. When she became pregnant, it was her first choice. But Janine, who was quite petite herself, was married to a football linebacker who, she said, came from a "family of giants."
>
> All she could think about was "a 5-foot, 11-inch girl with the name of Tina, and it just didn't fit." When she gave birth, her beautiful daughter weighed a robust 9½ pounds. "She didn't look like a Tina," Janine explained, "but she was a perfect Heather."

Even if the name Tina had been chosen and she had turned out to be tall, Janine would have then come to associate that name with height. But sometimes, the choice of names has more serious implications, especially when family members pressure new parents to name their baby after a deceased relative.

> When Shira was pregnant, she and her husband, Aaron, agonized about naming their child. Shira's father, whom she adored, was a fun-loving, affectionate man. But shortly before he died, he was imprisoned for fraud, leaving his family embarrassed and impoverished. Aaron's younger brother, a beloved member of his family, had committed suicide some years before, leaving the family in a chronic state of grief and remorse.
>
> Both families were thrilled at Shira's pregnancy. The

baby would be the first grandchild on both sides. Then the pressure started, with Shira's mother insisting that the baby be named for Shira's father, and Aaron's insisting it be named in memory of his brother.

"The pain was still too raw," Shira said of her father's imprisonment and untimely death. "I loved my brother, but every time I thought about him, all I felt was pain," Aaron said. They shared their feelings with their families, but that didn't stop the pressure. Both Shira and Aaron were only children, and their families kept reminding them that if they didn't carry on these names, no one else would.

As her last month rolled around, Shira and Aaron sought counsel from their rabbi. At the first visit, he suggested they go home, sit together in meditation, and consult their hearts. At the next visit, they were both in tears. "My heart is full," Shira cried, "I think about my father every day." Aaron, choked with emotion, nodded in assent. "My heart is also full. I carry my brother inside me, and I think about him with love."

"Then there is no need to name your baby for these people," the rabbi said. "They are in you, they are with you, and they always will be. But they still give you pain, and if you name your baby for them, that pain will find its way into the relationship that you have with your little one. You can look at photographs of your father and brother, introduce them to your baby, recall the fond memories you have and the love you feel. But give your baby his own name, or her own name—a name that gives you joy."

Until she gave birth, however, the family pressure remained. Once the baby was born, though, all was forgotten. Shira and Aaron decided to use the initials of her father's and his brother's name in naming their baby. But the name they chose gave both of them joy, and as the baby grew, she reflected that joy.

In choosing your child's name, try to consult your source of spiritual wisdom. If you need guidance, as Shira and Aaron did, consult someone whose opinion you respect. Most of all, think about the distinctive place in the universe that your precious little boy or girl will inhabit and about the lifelong pleasure that he or she will experience in having a name that fits—a name you have chosen with love.

Growing . . . and Worrying

While baby showers are underway, and you're deluged with advice and war stories, and you're choosing a name, Mother Nature is marching on, preparing you and your baby for labor and delivery. During the beginning of your third trimester, your baby undergoes dramatic growth and change, just as you do.

By the end of the seventh month, he is about 16 inches long and weighs about 3 pounds. Over the next eight weeks, your baby's height and weight grow markedly. In the last two months, in fact, there will be a weight gain of about an ounce a day.

As your baby grows, you, too, are becoming rounder and rounder. Powerful emotions may again rise to the surface. Some women feel awkward, even clumsy, about their changing shapes, and fearful that they have lost their femininity. A woman may worry about her sexual attractiveness and find herself feeling atypically jealous if her partner glances sideways at another woman, or hypersensitive if he is not exceedingly attentive to her.

As she feels her baby kicking up a storm every day, and as she contemplates the lifelong role of motherhood, she may experience a wide variety of emotions—some of euphoria, others of fear. During these last months, a woman's turning inward may deepen as she ponders or worries about her own health, the well-being of her baby, and the labor that lies ahead. Some women have bad dreams at this time, dreams that reflect worry about having a normal baby.

Many women wonder if they'll live through the labor and become preoccupied with thoughts of dying. Others convince themselves that they don't have the necessary parenting skills and won't know what to do after the baby is born. The fact that these thoughts are experienced by women all over the world—and always have been—does not diminish their impact for the individual woman who is going through them.

Now, more than ever, a woman needs understanding, empathy, and support. She needs people around her who comprehend the nature of pregnancy and the degree to which it affects the physical and emotional state of a mother-to-be.

In addition to feeling weighed down, you may experience shortness of breath and indigestion as your baby increases in size and puts pressure on your stomach and diaphragm. While physical signs are easy to see, it is not always easy for a partner to deal with moods and changeable emotions. If a woman is usually outgoing and bubbly and now becomes introverted or irritable, her partner may find himself reacting to the behavior of the moment and forgetting that moods are often a function of fluctuating hormones and/or the genuine anxiety that arises before labor and birth.

At this time, as at so many others, a woman and her partner need to give themselves the gift of spirituality, to find that special time each day or evening to be together with their baby and with God. These moments need not involve an elaborate ritual. You might choose to sit together in silence, or to discuss the things each of you is experiencing, or to contemplate the changes taking place in your baby's development, or to speak to your baby directly.

Once you enter this spiritual space, both of you will

know that God's spirit is infusing you and your baby with wisdom and love. That wisdom, that love, are contagious. In the quietness of spiritual meditation, when life-affirming thoughts rise to the surface and negative ones recede, the mother-to-be will feel comforted by being in the presence of a loving partner and a loving God, and her partner will allow all of his understanding and empathy to find expression.

Lamaze to the Rescue

This is the time to avail yourself of the important learning experience that will assist you through labor. Since 1960 in America, the Lamaze method of prepared childbirth has helped women and their partners understand the physiological aspects of labor and delivery and taught them the breathing exercises that facilitate both. Other methods—the Bradley method, to name one—have also become popular.

The term *prepared childbirth* was carefully chosen by the early practitioners of Lamaze. This is not natural childbirth unless, that is, you are having your baby in an open field without the assistance of a doctor or midwife. Neither is it painless childbirth, unless you receive regional anesthesia (generally, an epidural) in early labor or you are having your baby under general anesthesia (which is only given for emergency deliveries, since the potent gases of general anesthesia travel through the placenta to the baby). Childbirth and pain are so closely associated because— plainly and simply—labor and delivery involve pain.

But prepared childbirth is another thing altogether. The theory underlying this method is that knowledge diminishes anxiety and fear, and when each is lessened, the mind and body are better equipped to deal with the task ahead. We know this from less monumental examples than childbirth.

If we are well-prepared for a test, we have less fear and we perform better. If we know the ingredients of a recipe, its preparation goes more smoothly and the outcome is more predictable. If we map the route of a long trip, we are less apt to lose our way. So it is with the preparation involved in labor and delivery.

The best time to begin a childbirth preparation class is during your seventh month. Most teachers conduct a series of six classes, so signing up at this time will give you plenty of time to practice the exercises. If you are having your second or third or even eighth baby, one or two refresher classes will be helpful. In any case these classes will help you reclaim some control over childbirth. Knowledge really is power, and in these classes you'll be receiving the information and how-to strategies that will make you feel less fearful.

In most cases both a woman and her partner attend the classes. Any coach, however—a mother, a sister, a best friend—can fill the bill. Of course, it should be someone to whom you feel close and with whom you want to share this most memorable of life's experiences.

During your classes you will learn everything you want and need to know about labor and delivery: how to recognize the difference between the authentic signs of labor and those that signal false labor, how to time your contractions, when to call your doctor or midwife, and what untoward signs, if any, you should be alert to.

You will see graphic (and quite thrilling) pictures of the route that your baby will travel from its protective home in the uterus and bony pelvis down the birth canal and through the cervix to the outside world. In addition to being thrilling, however, these depictions may cause you to exclaim, as many women have, "How is this baby ever going to get out of me?" You will learn this, too.

You will learn how the contractions of the uterus (which is a muscle) serve to propel the baby downward as, at the same time, the soft tissues of the cervix are thinning out (or effacing) and also dilating (or stretching and growing wider) in centimeter increments to allow the baby to pass through.

You and your labor coach will learn that during the first stage of labor, the cervix dilates to 10 centimeters; during the second stage, your baby will be born; and during the third stage, the placenta (or afterbirth) will be delivered. But just as you're saying to yourself, "That's it?", you will learn that the first stage of labor is divided into three phases—those most people think of as "labor."

The first phase is the easy part and involves tolerable discomfort as the cervix dilates to 3 centimeters. During the second, more active phase, the cervix dilates to 6 centimeters, and your discomfort will increase. And in the third phase—hard labor—the cervix dilates to 10 centimeters.

All of these facts will fascinate you. The breathing exercises, however, that will help you negotiate the pain of labor will comfort you. Fernand Lamaze, a French obstetrician, was greatly influenced by an English doctor, Grantly Dick-Read, who wrote *Childbirth without Fear.* Both predicated their methods on the importance of a woman's knowledge about labor and childbirth, and the utilization of that knowledge to generate relaxation and thus productive and effective labor—free of fear.

The Lamaze method, as you will learn in your classes, calls upon many senses to bring about such relaxation. By focusing your eyes on a single spot, effleuraging (or massaging) your abdomen, and listening to your coach's breathing instructions, you will use the senses of sight and touch and hearing.

As each contraction begins, you will learn to employ these exercises automatically, literally blitzing your system with sensory stimuli that will travel directly to the center in your brain that perceives and reacts to pain. The pain of contractions will be competing to reach that pain center, but by faithfully focusing your eyes, effleuraging, and following the breathing patterns, you will be literally beating that pain to your brain.

Will the Lamaze method eliminate the pain? No. It takes powerful contractions to push a 6- or 7- or 8-pound baby into the world, and that hurts. Will it make the pain manageable or tolerable? Yes. And the amazing thing is that, much like transcendental meditation, you don't have to believe in the method to experience its salutary effects.

This is not to say that a woman must rely solely on this prepared method of childbirth to navigate her labor. Each person has a different pain threshold; one may be so high that root canal is tolerable without a shot of novocaine, another so low that combing one's hair is painful. Modern obstetrics also employs a variety of low-dose analgesics and regional anesthesia for those who need it. In addition, many pregnant women avail themselves of hypnosis and become so adept at autosuggestion that they manage labor with no medication at all.

Partners in Parenting

All this may seem so physical as to preclude even the mention of spirituality. Nothing is further from the truth. One of the most powerful allies that a woman can have in labor is a coach who appreciates the power of spirituality.

Shanika, with her partner Tookie, enrolled in Lamaze class in her seventh month. "Whenever I get scared," Shanika told me, "I can't concentrate, so I usually don't hear anything that is being said. I was so afraid of giving birth that I thought the classes would be a waste of time." Tookie, who was an emergency medical technician, was not at all squeamish, so

Shanika trusted him to translate what the Lamaze teacher was saying. During their third class, the teacher mentioned that labor was best perceived not as a lengthy process, but one that involved just one minute at a time.

Tookie latched onto that concept and when he and Shanika were alone, he reminded her of it. "I was blocking so much out," Shanika said, "but he kept repeating it, and it finally reached me. It seems the first thing I was ever taught was that there was one God. And I was born on the first of February, so there was another one—I always considered it my lucky number."

For 2½ months, Shanika and Tookie practiced the breathing and pushing exercises every night for 10 minutes. Instead of invoking the typical directives— focus your eyes, take a deep cleansing breath, breathe in slowly—Tookie began each practice session with a prayer. "Dear God," he said, "We are one couple, having one baby. We will be going through one labor on one special day in the near future. We pray that our one experience will be easy and that it will take Shanika only one minute at a time for her to get through it."

Of course, they, like other people, could not predict what their experience would be like. But for the months they practiced at home, Shanika felt a growing sense of peace and confidence. "By the time our last class came around," she said, "I had so completely begun to think of labor as 'one minute at a time' that I had lost my nervousness. I told everyone in the class about it, and they laughed and said, 'Good luck' and 'keep believing it,' but, for me, it made all the difference."

Sally and Manuel utilized spirituality in another way:

Each night, they would begin their Lamaze practice sessions by creating the kind of atmosphere that they hoped would prevail in their home after their baby was born. First, they chose their favorite music and played it softly in the background. After dimming the lights, Manuel massaged Sally's shoulders, then her hands and feet, and they both spoke to their baby, expressing how lucky they felt to be helping their little one into the world.

Instead of having Sally focus on a remote spot, Manuel gazed directly into her eyes as he guided her to effleurage, take a deep cleansing breath, breathe in slowly through her nose, and exhale slowly through her mouth. When it came time to practice pushing, Manuel positioned himself in front of Sally and placed her feet on his shoulders, encouraging her strenuous efforts. And after their practice sessions, they would pray for their child's health and, of course, an easy labor.

Like Shanika and Tookie, they had no idea how labor would progress. But in concentrating on their relationship and on the task at hand, they, too, were embracing the very essence of spirituality—living in and appreciating the present, including the loving bond that they had already established with their baby and with God.

Talking with Your Baby before Birth

Manuel told me that he had been persuaded to begin speaking to his baby before its birth when he studied ancient cultures and learned that Greek noblewomen surrounded themselves with everything beautiful while they were pregnant. They believed, he said, that "every sight, every taste, every sound directly influenced their unborn children—and when you look at the magnificent Greeks that they produced, it's obvious they were right." At first, he said, Sally found this strange, but was soon "having long conversations with our little gem."

Yet, not everyone arrives at this kind of communication by the same route. A woman named Patti came to meet her baby, not through the inspiration of ancient history, but from painful disappointment.

Patti had been raised in a home that she described as very religious. So religious that before she decided to become an elementary school teacher, she had contemplated entering a religious order. She told me that her whole life had been shaped and enhanced by her religion and that "for as long as I remember, I've been praying to God."

So it was quite upsetting to Patti that, when she became pregnant with her first child, the relationship she had to prayer and to God seemed to change abruptly. "The first thing I did when I found out I was pregnant was to go to church and light a candle and thank God for this gift," she said. "But as my pregnancy went on, prayer just didn't seem to work. It didn't seem to be enough to express how I felt."

This turn of events upset Patti; she felt that a central piece of her life was missing, and she had no idea how to replace it. Then, she "sort of accidentally" discovered the answer. In her second month of pregnancy, she was sitting alone in her living room listening to her favorite recording of a famous French singer crooning romantic ballads.

"I usually listened to that music with my husband and sang along or pointed out a particular lyric to him," she said. "But he wasn't there, so I just started stroking my stomach and talking to my baby. 'Listen, sweetie,' I said, 'do you like this music? Would you like me to sing it to you?' It was strange. Here I was, speaking to a baby—an embryo—I had never seen, but I felt I was being heard. It was almost mystical."

From that day on, Patti spoke to her baby regularly, asking him (it did turn out to be a boy) how he liked a particular food she had eaten, if the exercise class she had taken was too strenuous, how he felt about taking a long car trip. She explained things to him, comforted him when she felt under the weather, and sang to him as she cleaned her home.

"I don't know how the universe works," she said, "but I do know that talking to my baby made me feel closer than ever to God. It wasn't prayer exactly, but I know God heard our conversations and I felt embraced and loved."

Patti told me that she had gotten to know her baby so well that she was afraid her husband, Tim, would be a stranger to their little one unless he, too, established the same kind of relationship. One evening, she encouraged Tim to talk to the baby and, to her delight, he was eager to do so. As the pregnancy progressed, they both started touching their little boy, feeling the outlines of his legs and head and backbone, laughing when they detected him curling up in his snug environment.

In speaking to their baby throughout the pregnancy, Patti and Tim had begun a lifelong bond with their little son. Actually, they were somewhat ahead of their time. Today, studies have indicated that babies do, indeed, hear in utero and respond to other stimuli as well. In fact, it is now believed that the life babies experience before birth plays a large part—perhaps the defining influence—in shaping human personality.

However you and your partner choose to communicate with your baby or to create your spiritual space will be *your* way. If it yields you peace and insight and a closeness to each other, to your baby, and to God, you will have succeeded in bringing a beautiful and life-affirming dimension to your pregnancy. And none too soon. As the eighth month arrives and you embrace the gift of spirituality, it will embrace you as well.

Chapter
Fourteen

Approaching the Finish Line
Your Eighth Month of Pregnancy

Could it be possible? A full seven months have elapsed and you are now entering the last two months of your very special and unique pregnancy. As you enter your eighth month, you may find yourself continuing to turn inward. You definitely will find yourself significantly more round. It may now be difficult for you to find a comfortable position to sleep and, generally, to feel any ease in getting around.

With your body preparing itself for birth, increased rest is important. While you rest, and even when you're not resting, your baby is continuing to grow by leaps and bounds. This is a major period of maturation for the little person who will soon become your son or daughter.

By the end of the eighth month, your baby will be approximately 18 inches long and weigh about 5 pounds. This weight gain adds an important layer of fat under the baby's skin, which helps keep body temperature at a constant rate after he or she has entered the world.

For reasons largely unknown, some women go into labor in their eighth month. Although a full-term pregnancy is obviously Mother Nature's goal, babies born at this time usually fare well. Their body weights are ample and their lungs are usually well-developed enough for them to thrive. In some cases, medical monitoring, medication, and bed rest can halt the progress of labor until the babies mature even further. Babies born earlier than 32 weeks are at higher risk for problems.

While you're going through each week of your eighth month and continuing—alone and together—to enjoy your spiritual space, include a special prayer for the continued health, growth, and safety of your precious cargo and for the wisdom to treat yourself with great care and solicitousness. Now is the time to slow down a little, even though this may seem impossible.

Guilt

By now, you have accustomed yourself to juggling a million things, including taking childbirth classes, perhaps decorating your baby's room, lining up a support system of help, trying to rest more often, and making plans to take some time off from work—all this in addition to holding a job. For a woman who works outside the home, this means traveling to and from work, meeting the demands of pressing schedules, fulfilling various and sundry responsibilities, and, after work, trying to race to the cleaners, pick up the mail, practice breathing exercises, and be a good mate in the few moments that remain of the day. Whew!

If holding a job means that you're home raising other children, you've been spending your days shopping for food, preparing and serving meals, making the beds, vacuuming and dusting and cleaning your home, driving your children to dentist and doctor appointments and music and dancing lessons and religious school instruction, and pursuing your own individual interests. Whew again!

Although women who prefer to stay home with their children are often criticized in today's make-a-buck world, I think that Mary Hollingsworth had it right when she said: "Most folks couldn't survive such a leisurely, *non-working* life of luxury."

But the modern woman, no matter what her choice, is often stuck between the proverbial rock and hard place. If she works outside the home, she feels guilty about leaving her baby in someone else's care. If she stays home, she feels guilty about not being a wage earner. If she can afford to stay home but prefers to work at her chosen profession, she feels both angry at staying and guilty at leaving. In other words, a modern woman can't win.

> *Lolly faced all of these issues. When she had her first child, Scotty, she was 19. Her husband, Frank, was a college graduate in his early twenties and had a good job. But, Lolly said, "I felt bad that he had to work such long hours and that I couldn't help out." Guilt.*
>
> *When Scotty was three and entered nursery school, Lolly enrolled in college and, after six years of undergraduate and graduate studies, became an accountant. During those years her mother took care of Scotty whenever Lolly was in classes and, after graduation, when she started work. "When I was in school," Lolly said, "I could still see Scotty off to school and be with him after school and most evenings. But when I started to work, I worried that I wasn't spending more time with him." Guilt.*
>
> *When Lolly became pregnant with her second child, she agonized over what to do: Stay home and feel guilty or go to work and feel guilty. Frank did well in his job,*

but in the almost 10 years between babies, economic times had changed and Lolly's income had become important.

In the middle of this dilemma, Lolly's boss offered her a raise and the chance to become a partner. At the same time her mother became seriously ill. "This was a monster," Lolly said. "I thought about how incredible it would be to rise in my career, while I also thought about how incredible it was to have had a really nurturing mother in my life. Then I thought that I was going to fall apart trying to decide which was more important."

Lolly said that she believed God intervened when a friend bought her a subscription to a magazine about women entrepreneurs. "It talked about blending motherhood and careers, and I almost didn't read it because I'm an accountant who deals with concrete, bottom-line things, and 'blending' sounded a little far-out. But when I opened it up, my eyes popped out. Here were successful women doing it all—being the kind of mothers they wanted to be and having the kind of careers they wanted to have."

After speaking about her decision with Frank, Lolly made her move. In the seventh month of her second pregnancy, she resigned from her firm, set up a high-tech accounting office in her home, and began to freelance. By the time her second son, Danny, was eight months old, she had a well-established accounting firm. "Every day, I eat breakfast with my sons," she said. "When Scotty comes home from school, I'm there. And when the baby cries, even though the baby-sitter is great, it's me who wipes his tears and it's me who gives him lunch and it's me who tells him Mommy loves him."

Not all women have jobs that will allow them the freedom to emulate Lolly. But, whatever your circumstances, try to seek ways through insight and prayer that allow you to rid yourself of guilt. Harmful guilt benefits neither you nor your child.

Sometimes, God's wisdom is conveyed through lessons that are right in front of you waiting to be interpreted, such as butterfly wings or a bend in a tree. At other times, wisdom arrives through an unlikely route, such as Lolly's gift subscription. Your mission, your challenge, is to see what life is telling you and to act on your insights in productive and life-enhancing ways.

As a woman navigates her last two months of pregnancy, however, even obvious things may be obscured. At this time, it is not uncommon for a woman to flop down in the middle or at the end of the day and wearily exclaim, "It's all too much." But don't worry. Everything will get done. This is yet another time when communing with God can guide your actions and help you to set intelligent priorities. There's a wonderful Yiddish folktale that can serve as a guide to establishing priorities.

Take in a Cow

A widow ran desperately to her rabbi to tell him that she lived in one room with her young son and that a relative now wanted to move in. "Take in a cow," the rabbi told her. The widow was completely mystified by this advice, but not wanting to question the rabbi, she complied.

The next week, she ran again to the rabbi to say that the relative still wanted to move in, but now she had her son and a cow in the one room. "Take in a goat," said the rabbi. Again, reluctantly, she complied. The same scenario went on for weeks and weeks, and every time the widow complained about the relative's imminent arrival and the fact that her son and the animals now took up all the space in their one room, the rabbi suggested taking in another animal.

The last time the widow visited the rabbi, she was simply desperate. "Rabbi," she said, "I am living in one room with my son and a cow and a goat and a chicken and a dog and a cat and two birds, and my relative still wants to move in."

"Let out the animals," said the rabbi. And when the widow let the animals out, she felt as if her one-room home were a spacious palace and that having only one relative move in would be the easiest thing in the world.

Especially during the last trimester of pregnancy, all of us have felt as overwhelmed as this woman. So take the rabbi's advice: Let out what is not necessary to keep in. Once you simplify your life in this way, you, too, will have more space.

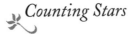 *Counting Stars*

Karen arrived at the same conclusion, "not one second too late," she said. The senior editor at a distinguished publishing firm, she was accustomed to attending six decision-making meetings a day, juggling four urgent telephone calls at one time, reading mail and faxes that required answers yesterday, and flying around the country to attend various publishing seminars.

As her first pregnancy progressed, Karen began to feel overwhelmed. "I was used to the demands of my job," she said, "but when I started to think about all that I had to accomplish to prepare for the baby's birth, it all seemed to much. I'm the kind of person who has to dot every i and cross every t. I just can't do things halfway."

Karen said that she had once seen a funny plaque. "It's significant that I memorized it. It said, 'Right now, I'm going to have a nervous breakdown. I've planned for it, I've worked hard for it, and no one's going to stop me from having it.' At first it seemed amusing, but all of a sudden, it was scary—I really felt that way."

Karen's husband, Lorenzo, had a very different temperament. Although a successful entrepreneur, he went through life with a whimsical sense of humor and, she said, "never dotted an i or crossed a t." When Lorenzo noticed how stressed out Karen was, he thought of an original way to help her. One evening, they were eating dinner at a seaside restaurant, gazing through the window at the night sky. "Let's count the stars," he said, and started to count out loud. "One, two, three, four, five. . ." Pretty soon, they were both laughing at the ridiculousness of such an impossible thing.

A few days later, they attended an opera. "Let's count the seats," Lorenzo said, and again began with "one, two, three. . ." The next week, they decided to plant some impatiens and Lorenzo said, "Let's count the flowers." At dinner that night, he suggested that they count the grains of salt. But Karen didn't get it and finally shouted, "Everything you want to count is impossible. Why are you suggesting these things?"

"Because there are so many of them," he explained, "that if I don't start counting them now, I'll never get to the end."

"But you'll never get to the end," she cried. "If you want to count things, why not choose fingers or car brands or even jigsaw-puzzle pieces—things that have a limit? If you count the stars or flowers or grains of salt, there will always be millions of others that you haven't counted."

"That's right," Lorenzo smiled. "Just like the meetings and phone calls and letters you think you have to respond to immediately. They'll always be there, and there'll always be others, so why not set yourself some limits?"

Karen couldn't get this idea out of her mind. Over the next several weeks she found herself daydreaming about the zillions of stars in the sky, the countless grains of salt, and all the other uncountable things that Lorenzo had suggested they spend their time enumerating. Unconsciously, she found herself responding differently to the demands of her job, cheerfully telling her coworkers, "This can wait, that will get done." To her astonishment, she realized that she worked even more efficiently and felt less frenzied and pressured.

"I even brought this attitude to my pregnancy," she said. "It became clear to me that there would always be something else to do and that I could stop counting up my accomplishments and start to enjoy each task."

Over the years, Karen and Lorenzo became the parents of three children. "When I look back at that first pregnancy and remember how frazzled I was," Karen laughed, "I realize what a great lesson I learned from counting the stars. It certainly helped me with my job, but not half as much as it helped me be a mother. That is really a job with no end of things to do, but whenever I felt overwhelmed, I'd just go the cabinet, take out the saltshaker, and say to myself, 'Start counting.'"

Setting Priorities

Insight and change come from many sources. The widow learned to let out the cow. Karen learned to count stars—and salt. Both of them learned to see things in new ways and to establish realistic priorities. If you have not already initiated a plan that will allow you to set limits and conserve your energy, the following list may be helpful.

❧ If you plan to continue working outside the home, start a diligent search for your baby's surrogate caretaker as early as possible. Interview people, get references, and trust your instincts. When you're away from home, you'll feel good knowing that the person taking care of your baby is warm and caring.

❧ In the same way, interview one or two pediatricians before you give birth, either in person or by phone. Most women want the doctor who will care for their baby to be accessible, both emotionally and geographically.

Ask if the doctor makes house calls, evaluate the friendliness of the office staff, find out how the doctor can be reached in an emergency, learn if he is covered by your insurance program. Again, trust your instincts and don't forget that if your caretaker or pediatrician doesn't work out, you can always make a change.

❧ Make sure to schedule childbirth classes near your home. If they're in the evening, try to take off the afternoon from work. If possible, schedule them for the weekend; many childbirth teachers will accommodate this request.

❧ If you're a first-time mother and feeling insecure about your parenting skills, by all means take a class. Many are offered in hospitals or community centers. Or, if you have a friend who is an experienced mother, don't hesitate to ask her to show you exactly how to give a bath, change a diaper, or burp a baby. Once you have a little hands-on experience, your anxiety will vanish, so don't deny yourself this very important learning experience.

❧ If you are buying your baby's layette, make a list of everything that you'll need beforehand. Ask someone with experience which things are absolutely necessary (don't forget, you'll be getting many gifts of layette items). Think about ordering items through a mail-order catalog. If you're not satisfied, they're easy to return.

✸ Today, most women stay in the hospital after birth for only one to two days, so you don't have to pack your overnight bag elaborately. Usually, a nightgown and robe, some slippers and some toiletries are sufficient. But you can really put this on the back burner, since your partner or a family member can always bring you what you need.

✸ As for decorating your baby's room, this is absolutely not a high priority. This can be a fun project, if you have the time and energy. But if you're simply too busy to get all those extra, adorable things before you deliver, they can certainly be purchased over a period of months—even with your little one in tow. All you really need is a cradle or crib, a changing table, and the requisite supplies from the drugstore (such as diapers, lotion, powder, and cotton swabs).

✸ I believe that buying yourself a rocking chair is as important as buying a crib for your baby. This old-fashioned piece of furniture can be the best friend that a new mother has—both comfortable and comforting, especially for those 2:00 A.M. feedings.

✸ Don't leave your support system to chance. Everybody's busy, so the people you're depending on to be there for you may be busy at the very moment you need them the most. Well before you give birth, speak to the people who have offered help or to those you believe will be available.

Be specific: "Can I count on your helping me out for 2 hours every Saturday morning?" Or "After I go back to work, will you be able to pick up my dry cleaning when you get yours?" Also, try to line up reliable delivery people from the grocery store, pharmacy, even restaurants.

❧ The most important, but possibly most difficult, priority is for you to find the time for a little extra rest during your third trimester. If you're pulled in 20 directions, this may seem completely out of the question, but it's not.

If you commute to work on a train, take this time to meditate: Clear your mind, take some deep breaths, recite a mantra, and close your eyes. Even 5 to 10 minutes of such an exercise can have a wonderful effect on your nervous system (and, by association, on all your other systems and on your baby's).

If your work environment is like a zoo, make a point to take 5 minutes out of every hour to do the same thing, even if it requires you to escape to the rest room. Don't forget, 5 minutes is only 300 seconds. If you do this exercise during the 8 hours of your workday, that is 40 minutes of rest. You deserve that and so does your baby.

❧ When you get home from work, eat slowly and try to get to bed early. Even if you're leafing through magazines or watching television or doing paperwork for your job, the very fact that you're in a reclining position will provide you with some of the rest you need.

❧ Well before you give birth, speak to your employer or employees about the time you plan to take off. If you are employed, make sure that you understand your firm's terms of maternity leave.

If you are an employer, chances are that you'll be

involved in your business on a daily basis, even if you're not on the premises in the last few weeks of pregnancy. If you don't have a fax machine in your home, this is a good time to get one. Set aside a specific time every day when your office manager can call you so you won't be interrupted at inconvenient hours of the day. After you give birth, this time may change as your baby's schedule does. Some babies are natural "larks," who awaken early and stay awake all day long, while some are natural "owls," who just love staying up all night.

If you are the kind of person who constantly thinks, "I should do this" and "I have to do that," it won't be easy to slow down and let some things go. But now is the perfect time to start viewing your pregnancy through a spiritual lens. Besides, setting priorities is exactly what parenthood will require of you.

When you need to cut back on your activities, especially if it's hard for you to say no, try praying for wisdom. No one really knows the mechanism of prayer or why some things that are consciously striven for fail to materialize while prayer seems to bring them about. But like anything that you are receptive to—a good idea, a beautiful melody, the aroma of a rose, a warm hug—prayer is remarkably effective in bringing about change. For women, particularly, who are so intuitively knowing, a receptivity to prayer is practically innate.

If there is one guiding mantra for the end of the eighth month, it is *simplify*. Here are some doable strategies.

❧ Spend your time only with people who make you feel good, who are supportive and understanding. Socializing, even with those with whom you feel comfortable, is exhausting. Talk itself can be depleting.

If, before this time, you have wanted to—but haven't—cut back on or eliminated a relationship that is irksome or tiresome or offers you only criticism, now is the time.

> *Before she got pregnant, Dani got so fed up with herself for associating with people who didn't make her feel good that she took an adult-education course entitled "Say What You Mean."*
>
> *"I must have been ready for the course," she told me, "because I started to put it to use right away."*
>
> *She started by responding to telephone solicitors. "I know you have a difficult job," she would tell them. "But I'm not interested in your product, so please go on to your next call." When they continued with another tactic, she said, "Please don't force me to hang up on you. Thank you for calling." The result was magic. "I meant what I said, and my voice must have reflected it. I was polite because that's my style, but I was also firm."*
>
> *So pleased was she by this success, Dani started to use her newfound ability to say what she meant with friends and family members. "One of my friends thought it was her duty in life to tell me what I was doing or saying or wearing wrong. 'Are you saying this to help me?' I would ask her. That's one friendship that went by the wayside because she wasn't."*
>
> *During her pregnancy, Dani, now practiced in the art of saying what she meant, found it easy to simplify her relationships. If she didn't feel like socializing, she would say, "I don't feel like socializing right now." If she wanted to get off the phone, she would say, "I'd rather speak with you another time. I know you understand."*
>
> *"I used to tolerate things that made me depressed and angry at myself," Dani told me. "The amazing thing that I learned was that being direct and honest improved my life and my relationships."*

✺ Get rid of it. In just a few weeks your home will be filled with your baby's new furniture, supplies, and gifts. So if you find yourself dusting an old bureau or looking at a pile of clothes that you planned to give away, call the Salvation Army now. In someone else's life, these may be a blessing; in yours, they are clutter. I know a highly productive woman who also manages to keep a remarkably neat home. I saw her philosophy of life etched in calligraphy and, of course, neatly framed on her office wall: "Outer Order, Inner Order."

✺ Plan ahead. As your due date nears and your need for rest increases, the ordinary activities of life may loom as burdensome tasks. Even making dinner may seem difficult. But if you spend 15 minutes planning your weekly menu, simplifying it to include easily prepared dishes and making sure that you have shopped for all the ingredients at one time, meals will be easy. Try to set up your doctor, dentist, or sonogram appointments all for one morning, the better to get them out of the way.

Establish a rest period that is inviolable—phone off the hook, doorbell unanswered, fax machine bell turned down.

At this time, simplifying your life—letting out the unnecessary things—will allow you to conserve the precious energy that you need for labor, childbirth, and the challenging task of new motherhood that lies ahead.

Chapter
Fifteen

Nine Months and Counting
Father Time and Mother Nature

Nowhere is the need for patience more evident than in pregnancy. Where lives the woman who, after eight months of carrying a child, is not ready to give birth? That is the prevailing sentiment when a woman enters her ninth month. Having spent what may seem like years going to doctors' appointments, eating the right foods, enduring discomforts, seeing her shape change dramatically, practicing childbirth breathing exercises, and managing the exacting responsibilities of home and work, she now finds herself fixated on both the calendar and the clock.

"I'm ready," she will say to everyone who watches with sympathy as she struggles to get out of a chair. But Mother Nature disagrees. Unless for some reason the labor begins earlier than the typical 40 weeks, Mother Nature really does know better. Her wisdom, while unfathomable, has kept God's universe in perfect balance since the beginning of time.

The Weight of the World

I often wonder why human pregnancy is nine months long, especially when women are so often psychologically ready to give birth after eight months. What cosmic erudition, what inexplicable enlightenment guides this process? Perhaps the answer lies in God's flawless understanding of the human condition. If women, in fact, gave birth when *they* were ready, they might not be prepared for the overwhelming task of childbirth. For it is only in the last month of pregnancy that women truly feel the weight of the world within them, when one more day seems impossible to bear, and when the arduousness of labor comes not as a convenient choice, but as a blessed relief.

By the end of the ninth month the baby is now about 6 1/2 pounds (an average, of course) and about 19 to 20 inches in length. The cells of the baby's brain have greatly increased in number, and a zillion other physiological processes are continuing to take place, all in preparation for life's biggest miracle—the entrance of a new human being into the universe.

Now, sensing that an arduous trip lies ahead, the baby begins to "settle down" into the upper part of the mother's pelvis. He or she is now so big that there is less room to maneuver in the womb's sheltering environment. The thrilling movements that began as blips and flutters and then grew into lively jolts and kicks become quieter, although still obvious and discernible. As the days and then weeks of your ninth month elapse, you, too, begin to collect your strength.

Imagine. Nine months (actually 10 lunar months) have

gone by: 40 weeks. And in this relatively short amount of time, you have carried and nurtured and even had a relationship with a child who is and will be like no other person on Earth. In this time, you have wept with joy, cried with anxiety, fantasized, fought your fears, followed your regimens, and also managed to do everything you did before you got pregnant.

"Next Time, I'll Lie!"

But nothing you have done, or will do, will bring your labor on any more quickly than God intends. As the days and weeks creep by and your due date approaches, another phenomenon is bound to occur. Like the unusual appetites that some women develop during pregnancy, this occurrence is completely unanticipated—and often hard to take. This is the increasing number of phone calls you will receive each day from well-intentioned friends, neighbors, coworkers, and family members.

"Are you still there?" one curious person may ask. "Any signs of labor yet?" another may ask. "So what are you waiting for?" yet another may chime in. Just when you look forward to a few quiet hours, the phone rings again and, even if your answering machine is on, the urgency and concern you hear in the voices on the other end may compel you to pick up the phone or at least call back.

At the end of the day, you realize that you have spent a good part of your day on the phone telling everyone the same thing: "Yes, I'm still here. No, there are no signs of labor yet." And then the evening calls begin. Arrgghh. Only experience will inspire you to withhold this information in the future.

"I was so excited to be pregnant," Vanessa told me,
"that from the first second, the whole world knew."

Vanessa's revelation was greeted by excited squeals of delight, followed by the inevitable question, "When is your baby due?" Delightedly, she told everyone who asked.

A month before her due date, the calls began. "The guy at the local supermarket called me, my godmother called me, every single one of my five sisters and two brothers and their husbands and wives called me, and even their friends called me," she said. "My priest called me and my coworkers called me, even though I had just seen them at work, and my mother called five times a day. And when I went out to get gas for my car, the service station attendant asked me, 'So when's the big day?'"

A self-described "people pleaser," Vanessa said she gave everyone a progress report—what the doctor said, when her next appointment was, how she felt, and even a description of a transitory backache and her sudden urges for egg rolls.

"I knew that everyone cared about me, so I felt obligated to tell them each little detail, but in every conversation I heard about this one's horrible labor or guesses about whether it would be a boy or a girl, and I got so much advice that my head was swimming."

By the end of her ninth month, Vanessa was so exhausted from talking that she asked her husband, Peter, to tell everyone who called that she was sleeping. That's when the phone calls picked up. "I told Peter we should install six new phones and get some operators to answer them," she exclaimed. "It finally dawned on me that the stupidest thing I ever did was tell anyone my due date."

As it turned out, Vanessa was 10 days overdue. She described those days as a nightmare of phone calls. "I felt like moving to the woods," she said, "where there are no phones." After the birth, when she was home with the baby, her coworkers in the secretary pool—none of whom had yet become mothers—came to visit. As they listened avidly, Vanessa described every detail of her labor and delivery.

During the visit, one of her colleagues took the opportunity to make a very special announcement. "Practically no one knows this yet," she said, "but I just found out I'm pregnant."

After everyone squealed with delight and congratulated her, she turned to Vanessa and said, "Don't scare me, but tell me the most important thing I should know before I give birth."

"I have only one piece of advice," Vanessa said, "don't tell anyone your due date. Believe me, the next time I'll lie!"

By treating all people with affection and respect, Vanessa showed her spiritual nature. She responded generously to everyone who expressed interest in her, but, unlike Karen, she hadn't learned how to set limits. She did, however, learn from her experience. When she became pregnant for the second time and was questioned about her due date, her answer was simple: "Sometime in the summer, but the date's a surprise."

Conserving Your Energy

Forewarned is forearmed. If you want to avoid hundreds of phone calls when you enter your ninth month, choose a creative way to let your friends and family know how you are doing. Reword your phone message: "Hi. I'm feeling fine today, and I thank you for your interest. If anything happens, I'll make sure to let you know." If you decide to pick up the phone, try to limit yourself to a 30-second conversation, letting the caller know that you are trying to find time to rest. Talk is fun but also exhausting. As your due date draws near, try to remember the importance of conserving your energy.

During labor, every cell of your body, every hormone, every muscle, every system, every resource of strength, every power of concentration will be engaged in the task of bringing your wonderful child into the world.

The most predictable thing about the onset of labor is that it is completely unpredictable. Unless your labor is induced, and unless you have chosen your due date beforehand, only God knows when that magic moment will take place.

Robins, Cubs, Butterflies, and Full Moons

Have you ever watched a tiny robin wriggle out of a hatching egg, or a tawny lion cub emerge sleepily from its mother, or a luminescent butterfly burst forth from its hazy chrysalis? If so, no doubt you wondered why and how, at a particular millisecond in time, the process of bringing forth a new life begins. What chemical signals, what confluence of circumstances, conspire to initiate this mysterious process?

I asked myself this question on the very first day that I worked as a delivery-room nurse at a busy, university-affiliated hospital reputed for its high birth census. Baffled by the fact that so few patients were in labor, I asked an experienced nurse what accounted for the empty labor-room beds. Without hesitation, she replied, "Just wait 'til the full moon."

She explained that the moon controlled the tides of the ocean and also the tides of amniotic fluid. When the moon was full, she explained, "we don't have enough beds—our patients are in the halls." By the time I became a nurse, I was in my early thirties and a true believer in empiricism:

If I couldn't see it, I didn't believe it. Here, I had just completed studying biology, physiology, anatomy, microbiology, physics, biochemistry—all the sciences—and was being told that the onset of labor was controlled by the full moon.

My initial reaction was disbelief, but I must admit that years of working in that specialty area seemed to prove my colleague right and my skepticism wrong. Since I worked the night shift, I became particularly attuned to moons that were as thin as slivers as well as quarter moons, half-moons, and, of course, full moons. In less than six months, I found myself gazing at the sky as I drove to work, predicting—with amazing accuracy—just how busy our floor would be.

To this day, I don't know if my coworker's full-moon theory is scientifically valid. But since I have not learned of a more persuasive explanation, I must give her theory the respect it deserves. Yes, I have read about the chemical cues and hormonal hints and emotional catalysts that bring about labor, but they are no more convincing—and much less poetic—than are the tides of amniotic fluid.

The Real Thing—The Onset of Labor

Believe it or not, you really are ready for labor. While you may have thought this day would never arrive or, at the end of your pregnancy, wished it would come sooner, here it is. In just hours from its onset, you will finally meet your little one face-to-face for the first time. I must quote Patti here one more time. When she realized that she was in real labor, she said the first thing that flew out of her mouth was "Zowie!"

Among all the events that life has to offer, the labor that precedes your child's birth is certainly among the biggest of "Zowies!" Yes, it may be tiring and difficult and even frightening, but don't forget that the exertions of Olympic athletes, Nobel Prize recipients, and planet-orbiting astronauts never resulted in a more thrilling outcome.

By the time your labor begins, you will have taken all of your childbirth-education classes. But it's still a good idea to read a book or two about prepared childbirth and to practice the suggested exercises. Remember, knowledge diminishes anxiety. Knowledge is power.

This knowledge will prepare you for that real thing called labor. To some degree, you may have a preview of labor when you experience Braxton Hicks contractions, commonly known as false labor. These may take place throughout your pregnancy but, for the most part, are so mild that they lie outside your awareness. In the latter months of pregnancy, they may become more frequent and even uncomfortable. What distinguishes them from the real thing is that they are irregular and they go away.

It is important to know that the uterus is a muscle and, like all muscles, is capable of tightening up or contracting. If you flex the bicep muscle of your arm, you will feel the entire muscle grow hard. This is precisely what happens to your uterus when your real labor begins. If your stomach seems hard but you can indent it with your finger in any spot at all, this is not a contraction. If, however, your entire abdomen becomes hard as a rock, that is an authentic contraction. It is these regular—not intermittent—contractions that will help propel your baby through the birth canal.

Even before contractions begin, other signs may indicate that labor is on its way. A couple of weeks before they deliver, some women wake up to find that they feel lighter and that the shortness of breath they may have been experiencing as a result of their baby pressing on their diaphragm has vanished. This phenomenon is called lightening, or dropping, and signals your baby's initial descent, or engagement, into the pelvis.

At this time, or soon after, you may become aware of a

mucousy discharge, a sign that the mucous plug from the cervix, which has served as a barrier to bacteria, has become dislodged. As the cervix gets softer in preparation for labor, some of its tiny blood vessels may burst and bring about a "bloody show," which can vary from a few drops of blood to approximately a teaspoon's worth. Another sign that labor is right around the corner is the rupture of the bag of waters, which can manifest itself in a slow leak or a torrent of amniotic fluid.

In your case, none of these things may happen, but you may experience even more subtle signs of impending labor. Some women develop a low backache that radiates around to the lower abdomen. Others get a sudden spurt of energy, while still others feel uncharacteristically lethargic. I have met dozens of women who told me that just before they went into labor, they developed a ravenous appetite for Chinese food.

So how will you know if it's the real thing? The absolute, definitive sign of authentic labor—even in the absence of all others—is regular contractions that get closer together and longer in duration. For instance, you may notice that you have contractions every 15 minutes for an hour, each one lasting for 15 seconds. If you then get a contraction after 20 minutes and the next one is after 8 minutes—that is not labor. If, however, your regular 15-minute contractions become regular 12-minute contractions, and if they start to last longer (for 20 seconds instead of 15 seconds)—that is real labor.

Three things happen in early labor: your uterus contracts, your cervix thins out (effacement), and it also begins to open up (dilation). This process may have begun as early as your eighth month. In fact, on your last visit to the doctor or midwife, you may have heard that "you're 30 percent effaced and 1 centimeter dilated." It's always nice to learn that the process of labor has begun and you haven't felt a thing.

Typical first labors last 12 to 14 hours, so relax and take advantage of the last few hours before you will become a parent. This is a lovely time to sit with your partner, hold hands, and caress your baby. It is a lovely time to experience God's love and to feel that love and strength flowing into you. In between these beginning contractions, try to visualize this love traveling to every cell of your body, dancing through your veins on a ribbon of musical notes, filling your whole being like a million tiny star bursts.

More than vitamins or exercise or books or anything else imaginable, this love will strengthen and sustain you throughout your labor and delivery. Take it in. Absorb it. Retain it. It won't be long before the mysterious process of labor will escalate. But before this happens, take the time to say yet another prayer.

Dear God,
We thank you for bringing us and our baby safely to this
*   late stage of pregnancy.*
We ask that you give us the strength and fortitude to navi-
*   gate this labor with confidence and hope.*
We pray that you will guide and protect our baby's journey
*   so that he or she will enter the world unharmed.*
We trust in your love and wisdom.

This is also a good time to be inventive. Early labor will last many hours, so don't waste them sitting and watching a clock. If you feel perfectly okay and lack the patience to start breathing exercises, then find a funny television show. Laughter boosts the endorphins in the brain, and high endorphin levels are protective against pain. In fact, babies during the birth process receive endorphins from their mothers, yet another invisible process in which the mother protects her child.

Or turn on whatever kind of music makes you feel

good—anything from symphonies to serenades, from rock to rap. Or read aloud to each other, play cards, or fold the laundry. You may want to take a shower and wash your hair, shave your legs, and polish your nails. And don't worry about missing any of labor's progress. Mother Nature will tell you exactly when to slow down.

An Arduous Labor of Love
You're Not Alone

At the moment you realize that you're really in labor, you may suddenly realize that this monumental job is one you must do alone. "Oh my goodness," you will wonder, "can I really go through with this?"

The answer is an absolute, nonnegotiable yes, because you're not alone. With you at all times, available to be called upon at a moment's notice, is your true inner strength, the glittering riches that you have found in your spiritual center over the last nine months. And embracing you throughout your labor will be the invisible sources of strength that have guided women through labor since the world began: Mother Nature, Father Time, and the ineffable power and beneficence of God.

That beneficence has ordained that in the early part of labor, "ouch" will not be part of your vocabulary. Your contractions will be extremely tolerable, no more uncomfortable than the mildest of tummy aches, at the worst. Unless you are bleeding heavily or seeing a dark-colored amniotic fluid—in which case your doctor or midwife will suggest immediate hospitalization—you will be spending the next several hours alone together, timing contractions, finding a comfortable and comforting spot in which to sit or lie down, and, hopefully, enjoying some meaningful moments of spiritual harmony.

If this is your first baby, you will not be expected at the hospital until you are having contractions every 4 minutes for an hour. That means that you may be spending the entire first stage of labor—6 to 8 hours—at home. For your second or third or eighth child, you certainly won't wait that long, since the progress of any deliveries subsequent to the first are less predictable and may last anywhere from 20 minutes to 6 hours.

As the hours of labor pass, your contractions will get stronger and stronger. They may now be coming every 10 minutes and lasting for 30 seconds. During this time, you may not need the breathing exercises, but you might choose to do them anyway. Your task in early labor is to relax—to rest your system as much as possible for the more strenuous labor that will soon arrive.

You may be very happy at this point, realizing that while real labor is here, you're still quite comfortable, full of excitement, and almost bursting with optimistic anticipation. And this may last until you are completely, 100 percent effaced and 3 centimeters dilated. But how will you know?

"Ouch!"

As effacement and dilation progress, your contractions will get stronger, closer together, and more long-lasting. At one arbitrary point, you will feel the first real discomfort of a contraction. While other contractions may have inspired an "ooh" or an "aah," this will be your first "ouch." Instinctively, you will find a comfortable position and wait for the contraction to pass.

This turning point signals a change from the latent labor that you have experienced to the active phase of labor—the phase in which your cervix dilates from 4 to 6 centimeters and your discomfort or pain increases. It is at this point that all the preparation that you have done in terms of eye focus, effleurage, breathing exercises—and yes, Dad, coaching—will start to make a difference, and that you will be encouraged to go to the hospital or birthing center.

Going to the Hospital or Birthing Center

"This is it," you may murmur to yourself under your breath. As you start on your way, you may experience a combination of disbelief and anxiety. Even if you have toured the facility beforehand and seen what the admitting and labor and delivery rooms look like, it's not the same as going there as a woman in labor. This is for real and, yes, it can be scary. But that fear won't have much time to take hold because, even on the way to the hospital or birthing center, your contractions will keep you busy.

The admitting routine is pretty much the same in all facilities. First, you will change into one of those beautiful, "designer" hospital gowns. Then you will get weighed and be asked to provide a urine sample. Then you will be asked when your labor began and if you have eaten anything in the past 12 hours.

Most doctors will warn you not to eat if you think labor has begun because a full stomach can be dangerous in the unlikely event that you receive general anesthesia. Some practitioners, however, who eschew the use of intravenous drips with their high glucose content, encourage women to eat small portions of protein and carbohydrate foods and to ingest citrus fruits throughout labor, the better to maintain their energy.

After the nurse has listened to your baby's heartbeat, you and your coach will be ushered to your labor room, where an IV will be started, and you will be hooked up to a fetal-monitoring machine, which will monitor your contractions and your baby's heartbeat throughout labor. As all this takes place, you can still invoke the spiritual sensibility that brought you to this place in time. I was the privileged witness to such a scenario.

> *At three A.M. on a drizzly rainy night, Jeanne and Damon came barreling into the delivery room, she huffing and puffing, he serenely holding her hand. They were a most unusual couple—both ministers—and already the parents of two young sons. When I saw her into the admitting room, Jeanne was obviously in hard labor—with twins.*
>
> *Between her long, hard contractions, she and Damon held hands and prayed out loud. "Thank you, God," Jeanne said as she panted rapidly. "Thank you for helping me and my babies." To which Damon whispered, "Amen." I had seen women wearing headsets while in labor. One even sang an Italian aria as her baby was being born. But I had never seen, nor heard, a couple going through labor on the strength of prayer and, frankly, I was amazed.*
>
> *For the next couple of hours, as the labor grew harder and the contractions longer, Jeanne and Damon seemed positively joyful, praising God after every contraction subsided. Then, Jeanne was seized by a particularly painful contraction, and she lashed out at Damon and her doctor and the nurses. "I hate this," she shrieked. "What are any of you doing but standing around watching me suffer?"*

*At that—to everyone's surprise—Damon beamed at
his wife and put his hands together in a mock sign of
applause. "Isn't she beautiful," he exclaimed, and when
the contraction was over, both of them laughed and
Jeanne said, "These babies are just letting me know that
it's not any easier for them than it is for me. But God
made them fighters, so I have to be a fighter, too."
Within an hour, Jeanne delivered her two little fighters,
both girls.*

Although they had taken a Lamaze course, Jeanne and
Damon got through labor by focusing primarily on the
almighty power of God. Indeed, the effectiveness of the
techniques many women learn in their Lamaze classes depends a lot on their ability to focus, not only their eyes but
also their attention.

Visualization at this time can be very productive. For
instance, if you are able to picture the tissues of your cervix
smoothing out and getting thinner and the small opening
of your cervix beginning to enlarge, you will be concentrating so hard on the action that is taking place that you
may find the contractions elapsing in no time.

In the same way, if you picture your precious baby
moving forward micrometer by micrometer, collaborating
with you during these extraordinary moments, the image
may even make you smile. And, whether or not you went
to a hypnotist, you can imagine that your body is producing, along with hormones and chemicals, some kind of
magical agent—perhaps droplets of sparkling dew or a
graceful band of satin or even a phalanx of sturdy foot sol-
diers—that encircles your contractions and diminishes
your pain.

You will also be getting help from your doctor or midwife and from the nurses who staff the labor-and-delivery
area. But it is your coach—your partner, the father of your
baby—who will be your greatest ally. And even if the

baby's father is not present but another coach is with you, he or she will be your greatest ally.

There are some coaches, to be sure, who are intimidated by the hospital setting and also squeamish. But childbirth-preparation classes address these feelings in depth. Almost without exception, they disappear in time for a coach to be there for his partner in labor.

Another feeling—helplessness—may remain, however. Even when coaches are well-prepared and confident of their ability to assist the labor, they cannot anticipate how they will react to the sight or sound of the person they love crying out in pain. It is not easy feeling out of control, which is how many coaches feel when their best efforts don't seem to make things better.

> It was clear to me when Gordon and LuAnn came to my Lamaze class that Gordon didn't want to be there. When I asked the class what they hoped to learn, Gordon said, "How to control myself when I want to throw up." It was not that he was queasy by nature. A Vietnam veteran, he had seen frontline duty as, of all things, a medic.
>
> Over the next few weeks, when various class members had a chance to speak up, it became apparent that when it came to dressing a wound or splinting a fracture or stopping his car to help an accident victim, Gordon was the first to take charge. But the idea of helping his wife go through labor completely threw him. "What do you do," he asked, "when she's having pain and you're just standing there? You can't stop the pain."
>
> Gordon's anxieties touched the other coaches. As he spoke, many of them nodded in agreement. I tried to convey two concepts. The first one was that, to a very real degree, especially during hard labor, coaches were very much in charge. When women are going through transition, the hardest part of labor, they lose both their

ability to think logically, or respond to logic, and their sense of time. This is when the labor coach, who has not lost either of these faculties, becomes like a director of a movie. He calls the shots. Gordon liked that analogy; it reminded him of the training films that he had made during his service years.

The second point was that when, and if, a coach is not in control, his very presence serves to convey the strength that his partner needs to get through. Gordon liked that, too, as did the other coaches. The notion that helping their partners through labor didn't always require concrete action, that just being there was enough, seemed to place the issue of control in a more reasonable context.

As it turned out, LuAnn had a hard and lengthy labor which resulted, happily, in a 7-pound son named Lance. Gordon called me afterward to describe the labor at length and, quite proudly, to say, "It's a good thing I was there. I didn't really do much, but LuAnn keeps telling me how important it was that I held her hand. Imagine, I got through the whole labor without throwing up."

"I Can't Take It Anymore!"

As you progress through the second phase of labor and your cervix dilates from 4 to 6 centimeters, your contractions get closer together and increasingly powerful, lasting from 45 to 60 seconds. Now, your baby is moving downward with determination, pushing deeper into your pelvis. You're still hanging tough and so is your coach when, quite suddenly and seemingly with no preamble, another pivotal turning point arrives. In the words of a colorful client of mine, "This part ain't easy."

This significant shift in the course of labor is something

for which nothing can really prepare you—not a class, not a book, not another mother's description. All at once, Mother Nature brings profound changes to the mother in labor. Where one minute before, she may have been concentrating diligently on her breathing, she now experiences a torrent of symptoms that include transient nausea, involuntary shaking, an increased show of blood, and a radical change in mood.

Now, nothing is tolerable. The sound of a voice or the touch of a hand is unbearable. Offers of help are summarily rejected. And contractions become even more forceful, coming every 90 seconds and lasting the same amount of time. If there is one phrase—spoken in a thousand different languages—that characterizes how women feel during this phase of labor, it is "I can't take it anymore!"

If, however, you think of the labor process as one minute at a time, as Shanika did, you will survive it, as she did.

> *Throughout her entire labor, Shanika said, "Tookie kept repeating, 'One God, one minute, one God, one minute, one God, one minute,' and then I started saying it, over and over and over and over. And it was true. Even though my labor lasted 14 hours, it didn't feel that way. It really did feel like just one minute at a time."*

Nevertheless, it is a daunting experience for coaches to hear their partners say, "I can't take it anymore!" Now, everything they do seems for naught. Every effort, every attempt to coach, seems to fall on ears that do not hear. And when they introduce the logic they know to be true, that in less than an hour, this will be over, it is met with antagonism and disbelief. Time means nothing to the woman in transition. To her, as many a woman has said, "This will never be over."

It may be helpful here to remember Sally and Manuel,

the couple who drew on the example of Greek noble-women to create a harmonious pre-birth experience for their baby.

> *When Sally was in hard labor, she screamed at Manuel, "This isn't working. I just want to be knocked out!" But Manuel kept his cool. He continued to massage Sally's shoulders and gaze into her eyes as he coached her breathing. In between contractions, he softly hummed the music they both loved and, during the very hardest stage of labor, he placed a cool washcloth on her forehead and put ice chips on her lips to relieve the dryness of her mouth. After about an hour, it came time for Sally to push, and Manuel got up on the bed and placed her feet on his shoulders, all the while cheering her on, reminding her that "in just a couple of minutes, our new little love will be here."*
>
> *Their "new little love" was a beautiful, 7 1/2-pound daughter named Elena. After the delivery, Sally told Manuel that the most encouraging part of her ordeal was that he had not lost faith. Everything that he said and did reached her. "Even though I screamed out," she said, "I knew that God was present. His love was there in Manuel's eyes."*

As Sally and Manuel learned, transition—while the most difficult part of labor—is the shortest phase of the whole process, usually lasting for no more than an hour. This is when the cervix dilates fully, from 7 to 10 centimeters, and the baby, whose head has been deeply flexed downward to its chest, now hyperextends his head in order to negotiate (literally, to get around) the symphysis pubis, an internal bony structure in the mother's pelvis.

During this arduous phase of labor, it is important for coaches to keep their cool, as Manuel did, to become directors, to have confidence that their presence and their continued coaching—even in the face of resistance—is vital in maintaining their partner's morale.

Almost without exception, women—universally—react to transition in the same way. Since Eve brought forth children in the Garden of Eden, this is how it has always been. This is how it is in China, in New Zealand, in Norway, in Africa, in Israel, in France, in Spain, in every place where women give birth. This is how Mother Nature works. This is what God ordains. This is why children are so treasured and revered—because bringing them into the world is the hardest, most painful, most arduous, most frightening, and, ultimately, most rewarding work of all.

Push

Just when a woman thinks she really can't take it anymore, and just when her coach might begin to think the same thing, the baby puts pressure on the mother's anal sphincter, and she feels the overwhelming urge to push. Within a few minutes, another dramatic change takes place. Hard labor is over. Just like that, it ends, and all the symptoms that attended it seem to vanish into thin air.

But that is not the end of labor, nor of hard work. Now, the last mile must be negotiated—pushing your baby into the world. A few years ago, I saw a fascinating film that depicted a baby's role in being born. It demonstrated that babies really do collaborate with their mothers in the process of birth, and it reinforced the immense role that spirituality can play in establishing the relationship between mother and child before birth.

The film revealed a baby during labor using its own muscles and lust for life to thrust forward with each contraction. The baby played an active role. Taking signals from each contraction, or perhaps initiating each contraction—which comes first, the chicken or the egg?—the baby appeared to make a conscious effort to help the mother.

Actually seeing the cooperative, synchronized exertions of both mother and baby transformed my vision of the birth process. No longer did I view it as a unilateral pursuit in which mothers labored alone. To this day, I cannot confirm that this collaborative process is the norm, but the very idea that—before birth—both mother and baby are working so purposively together is so lovely, so emblematic of the closeness that may ensue between mother and child after birth, that I carry it with me as a hoped-for truth.

Chapter
Seventeen

Giving Birth
A New Life, A New Love

When the time comes to push, women intuitively know and exultantly rejoice that the end of labor is near. They know that in a mere hour or two, their tireless efforts will affirm (and redeem) everything that they have endured. And, because hard labor with its unrelenting demands is over, they can concentrate with clarity on propelling their baby through the birth canal.

But pushing "ain't easy" either. If this is not your first baby, this stage of labor may only last 30 minutes, or 2 minutes. But since only God knows the length of each stage of labor, no man- or woman-made theories can predict for sure how long any will last. For first-time mothers, pushing usually takes 1 to 2 hours.

There are no rules. Except, that is, for a cesarean delivery, a surgical procedure in which the baby is lifted from the uterus. C-sections are either planned in advance or take place as a result of fetal distress that is picked up on a monitor, a sluggish labor that doesn't progress, or a disparity between the large size of a baby's head and the relatively small size of the mother's bony pelvis. In any of these scenarios, or in other rare and more drastic cases, a woman in labor is not called upon to push.

A Few Wisps of Hair

The pushing process is arduous and exhausting. How could it be otherwise? It will take all of your concentration and all of your energy. And then—oh my goodness—the baby begins to make his or her appearance. Slowly, a few wisps of hair appear as the baby's head starts to emerge. If you are pushing like Sally did, with her feet firmly pushing against Manuel's shoulders, your coach will see those little wisps first. When his eyes light up, when you hear him gasp in delight and astonishment, you will know that within minutes, your already beloved baby will arrive.

If you are delivering in a birthing center, you will deliver in the same bed in which you have labored. If you are delivering in a hospital, you will be taken to a delivery room. Over the table is a large light on which a mirror is attached. You may be too busy pushing to remember to ask for the mirror to be positioned so that you can watch the birth—so make it a point to remind your coach before labor begins to ask that the mirror be positioned properly.

Why should you miss seeing this once-in-a-lifetime sight? It's even better than the picture worth a thousand words. Actually, it's one picture for which no adequate words exist. Today, increasing numbers of hospitals allow cameras and camcorders in the delivery room. If yours does, snap or film away. You'll be watching this film when you are sitting in a rocking chair with your grandchildren.

Birth will now be only a few minutes away. But even before giving birth, you have already begun to appreciate the prophetic words of Elia Parsons, who said, "Nothing else will ever make you as happy or sad, as proud or as tired, as motherhood." In carrying your baby for nine months and, now, in laboring to bring your innocent infant into the world, you have already been called upon to be wise and strong and protective.

You have already experienced the powerful emotions, the physical rigors, the anxiety and joy that will be part of your parenting journey. This preparation for parenthood, this dramatic dress rehearsal, is further evidence of God's flawless design. Knowing that parenthood will require your most formidable resources, God fashions pregnancy and labor to allow a mother to glimpse the future, to see the challenges that lie ahead.

And you are already incorporating into your very being the insight of Emma, the quilter, who had learned that "nothing wonderful comes to you without at least a little difficulty." Now, seconds remain before you enter the second stage of labor—birth. This is the very essence of a labor of love, one of many you will expend for your child.

Too Tired for Love

For all of this time, your baby has nestled beneath your heart, swimming in the warm nutritious fluids of your womb. During every second of those months he or she has depended on you for life itself, and you, knowing this, have done your best to make sure those priceless seconds were safe.

Now, as you confront the last moments of labor, your baby faces them as well. In just a twinkling, you'll be making the most huge, muscle-wrenching, give-it-all-you-got push of your life—the push that thrusts your baby's head into the world. You'll be talking about that push for years to come. But before you recoup from this enormous effort, another contraction occurs, and you perform the second biggest push of your life—to deliver your baby's shoulders.

And then out comes the rest of the baby, wrapped in love and tied with heartstrings. All at once, the room resounds with a squalling and wailing that eclipses any aria sung by the likes of Pavarotti. There is your baby. There is your bundle of love. True love. Unconditional love. Concerned love. Protective love. Self-sacrificing love. But it is also a love that, because of the chaos of the moment, you may not feel immediately.

> When Valerie gave birth, she anticipated being swept away with the love that she had felt for her baby since the second she learned that she was pregnant. "I knew this moment would be the bright beginning that I had envisioned for my child," she said. "The thought of giving birth never even scared me, because I knew it would be worth everything."
>
> A spiritual person, who said she "learned life's great lessons from nature," Valerie brought her own picture with her when she went into labor, so she could focus her eyes on "a lovely image and a lovely thought." The picture depicted a graceful weeping willow tree surrounded by doves in flight and a radiating sun. "I focused my eyes on the sun," she explained. "I had already memorized the words."
>
> Throughout her rather difficult labor, the memory of those words kept Valerie's spirits up: "Hundreds of stars in the pretty sky, hundreds of shells on the shore together, hundreds of birds that go singing by, hundreds of flowers in the sunny weather. Hundreds of dewdrops to greet the dawn, hundreds of bees in the purple clover, hundreds of butterflies on the lawn, but only one mother the wide world over."

"I believed every word," she said. But when she entered hard labor and then pushing, she had a rough time. Both took longer than the books said they would, and by the time she gave birth, she was completely depleted. "I was so exhausted that when I heard the baby cry, I started to cry—but not from joy, from relief."

When the nurses brought Valerie her baby to hold for the first time, she said that "all I could do was stare into space. I had dreamed about this moment all my life, but when it happened, I told the nurse I was too tired to hold the baby. The only thing I felt was numb."

While Valerie was being taken to the recovery room, her husband, Matt, had a chance to hold their little daughter. It was not until a few hours later, after Valerie had gotten some sleep, that she got to meet and hold her "Sweet Sarah" at last. When she did, "everything I had imagined came true. I fell totally in love."

Valerie's experience is not uncommon. Labor and delivery are draining and, immediately after giving birth, many new mothers don't respond as they think they should. It takes them a little more time to fall in love.

"Hello, Baby, Welcome to the World"

Nevertheless, the drama taking place in the delivery room is pretty much universal. As your baby sings a lusty tune, you will hear three little words that will fill you with awe and wonderment. "It's a boy!" or "It's a girl!"

Up to this point in your life, you may have thought that "I do" were the most important words in the world. But even if you have known for months what the gender of your baby would be, these three words will be emotionally and spiritually energizing. A son. A daughter. Your son.

Your daughter. Most definitely another "Zowie" moment.

At the birth of their child, both the religious and the atheistic, both the poetic and the inarticulate seem to summon up the same words: "Oh my goodness, I can't believe it." These will be your words as well, yet another acknowledgment that this, the most awe-inspiring moment of your life, is of God's doing. As you stare in wide-eyed fascination at your new little son or daughter, you will hardly be aware that you are going through the third stage of labor, the delivery of the placenta.

"Who has red hair? . . . Look at that little cleft in his chin. . . . God, she's beautiful." Your words will tumble out—joyfully, gratefully. Or you may have no words, just wonder. You'll watch with surging parental concern as the nurse suctions your little one's mouth, injects vitamin K, clamps the umbilical cord, places drops in the eyes, swaddles your baby in a warm receiving blanket, and then places your precious baby in your arms for the first time.

At this moment you will know that it was all worth it. All of the strain and struggle and toil you have been through—waiting to learn if you're pregnant, the nine months of pregnancy with all its attendant discomforts and anxieties, the fear of labor and the actual labor itself—all are forgotten. This selective amnesia is yet another of life's impenetrable mysteries, yet another reason to praise Mother Nature's gentleness and God's overarching wisdom.

As you and your partner murmur sweet nothings to your cherished cherub—"Hello, baby, welcome to the world"—as you trace the outline of your little treasure's nostrils with your fingers, place your lips gently on the baby's forehead, watch as this perfect infant's tiny hand clasps your own, you will know that this moment is what life—and the spirit of life—is all about.

It was Henry Ward Beecher who said, "We never know the love of a parent till we become parents ourselves.

When we first bend over the cradle of our own child, God throws back the temple door and reveals to us the sacredness and mystery of a father's and mother's love to ourselves." Even before you bend over your child's cradle, you will know this love.

As you marvel at toes that wiggle, knees that flex, eyelids that blink, dazzling dimples, downy skin, soft tendrils of hair, and lips that sweetly pucker, you will feel as you have never felt before the loving presence of God.

And you will know that, yes, you have just participated in the greatest, most significant of life's dramas—the gift of life.

Notes

Notes

Notes

Notes

Notes

About the Author

Photo by Susan Kravitz

Joan Swirsky is a health and science writer for the *New York Times* Long Island section, the recipient of seven Long Island Press Awards, and the author of seven other books. A former obstetrical nurse, she is a practicing, certified Lamaze teacher and psychotherapist specializing in women's issues. She and her husband, Steve, are the parents of three grown children and have a grandson, Julian.